Dear Mrs. Fitzsimmons

Tales of Redemption from an Irish Mailbox

Greg Fitzsimmons

Simon & Schuster

New York   London   Toronto   Sydney

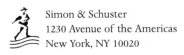

Simon & Schuster
1230 Avenue of the Americas
New York, NY 10020

AUTHOR'S NOTE:
Some of the names in this book have been changed. In some cases it is because
I describe close friends doing shitty things and they would sue me if they read this
(which most will not because they're fucking illiterates). See? Could have been a
lawsuit right there. In other cases I changed names because they were stupid.
Like my friend Julien. Always hated his name. Julien . . .

First Simon & Schuster hardcover edition November 2010

SIMON & SCHUSTER and colophon
are registered trademarks of Simon & Schuster, Inc.

For information about special discounts for bulk purchases,
please contact Simon & Schuster Special Sales at 1-866-506-1949
or business@simonandschuster.com

The Simon & Schuster Speakers Bureau can bring authors to your live event.
For more information or to book an event
contact the Simon & Schuster Speakers Bureau at 1-866-248-3049
or visit our website at www.simonspeakers.com.

Designed by Ruth Lee-Mui

Manufactured in the United States of America

10 9 8 7 6 5 4 3 2 1

Library of Congress Cataloging-in-Publication Data

Fitzsimmons, Greg.
  Dear Mrs. Fitzsimmons / Greg Fitzsimmons.
     p. cm.
  1. Fitzsimmons, Greg. 2. Comedians—United States—Biography. 3.
Television producers and directors—United States—Biography. 4. Television
Writers—United States—Biography. 5. Radio personalities—United States—
Biography. I. Title.
  PN2287.F525A3 2010
  792.7'6028092—dc22
  [B]
                                                        2010012113

ISBN 978-1-4391-8270-3

Permissions can be found on p. 211

Dedicated to

Bob Fitzsimmons (1940–1993)

Pat Fitzsimmons (1942–when she reads this book)

Erin Fitzsimmons

My pair bond, Owen & JoJo

and all the teachers who cared

Contents

Dear Mrs. Fitzsimmons

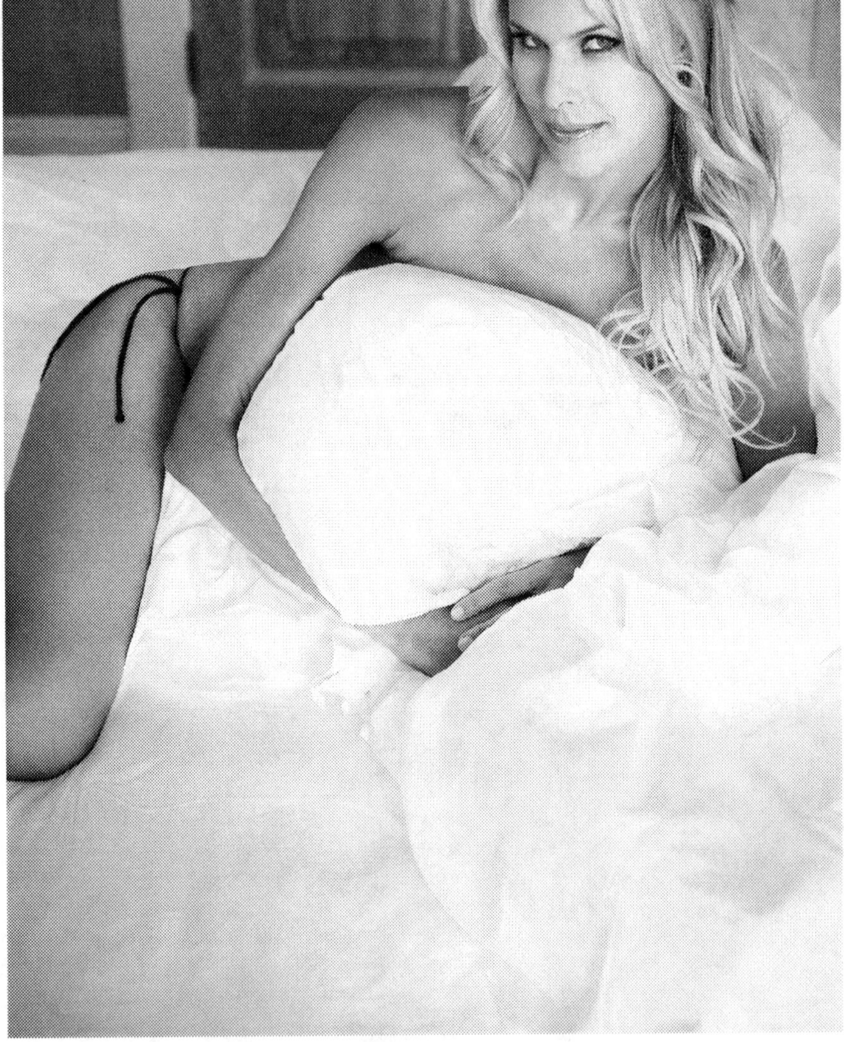

DONNA NEWMAN

Foreword by Howard Stern

As I am writing this, I have a gun in my mouth. I do not like writing forewords, and shooting myself seems like a better option. Forewords are a waste of time. People ask me to write these hoping my name will add value and sell the book. It's pointless. I've written them for Jackie "The Joke Man" Martling, Artie Lange, and Larry "Ratso" Sloman, and it didn't do a damn thing but diminish my book-forewording value on the open market.

Greg asked me to write this and stupidly I said yes because I have psychological problems and can't say no. I go to therapy three times a week and I still can't say no. So, as I am writing this my extremely gorgeous wife that I enjoy having sex with is upstairs alone. Every minute I peck away on these keys is time away from my wife's adorable vagina. Let's see: Fuck my stunning model wife, or write a foreword for Greg? To the left is a picture of my wife, just so you know what I'm talking about.

Okay, let's get on with it. I'm not going to lie to you, I have not read Greg's book, and I don't really know what it is about. Something about authority figures and not letting them shit on you. That's all I know. The best thing I can do here is to tell you how I feel about Greg.

Greg is just like sunshine. He's so sharp, so funny, so kind of bawdy. He brings so much to the character of Grandma Bunny. He's just the most charming performer in the whole ensemble, I think.

And that's how I feel about Greg. Actually, that's not how I feel about

Greg. It is how Sigourney Weaver feels about Betty White. I stole this quote off an audio tape of Sigourney Weaver doing a press junket for her new film. She was asked about her costar and I'm so lazy I couldn't even come up with my own adorable quote about Greg, so I just took hers. Even though these thoughts belong to Sigourney, it really is how I feel about Greg.

Now here are some of my original thoughts about Greg: A.) He is heaven on earth. B.) J. D. Salinger is a hack next to him. C.) I used to think Richard Pryor was funny until I heard Greg. Richard Pryor was so jealous that he lit himself on fire after he watched Greg.

Two other facts about our author you should know. 1.) Karen Carpenter laughed so hard during Greg's performance she threw up and killed herself. 2.) Michael Hutchins from INXS heard Greg's comedy CD and hung himself while masturbating.

All of that is not true but here's what is: Greg has a big penis. Really. Greg Fitzsimmons is also an outstanding comedian. He is a brilliant writer and performer, and should be a lot more famous than he is. He is so at ease on-stage, and I envy his ability to go up there and win a crowd over in seconds. I love him. You will, too. Greg, I do love you. I know that sounds fake, but I have a very warm feeling about you. There aren't many people I know that I'd almost invite over to my house. I care about you; I don't know why, I just do. You have balls of steel, and you are one of the funniest guests on my radio show. Thank you for endless hours of comedy, and congrats on getting the book deal you deserve. Now all of America will rejoice in your brilliance and avoid getting shit on by authority.

—Howard Stern

Prologue: How an Indiana Prom Launched a Literary Masterpiece

> A little rebellion now and then is a good thing.
>
> —Thomas Jefferson

The letter arrived in my mailbox two weeks after the performance. That particular night stood out from the mind-numbing succession of college shows I'd just performed in the upper Midwest. It had been one of those magic ones that make all the travel and loneliness worth it.

I was living in New York at the time, going to acting school during the day and performing as many as seven shows a night in the city. On a good night, after cab fare, I'd net about $60. The college shows helped make ends meet.

I'd fly to a city, rent a car, and then drive four hours to do a show that night, usually arriving about ten minutes before show time. Afterward, I'd be taken to a Bennigan's by the Student Activities members (usually headed up by the "gay Asian guy with a nose ring" and his best friend, "the Sad Girl"). Off to bed in a Motel 6, a wood block chained to the room key. Wake up the next day around seven, and by noon I am onstage in a student union cafeteria at a school two hours from where I'd been the night before. This would go on for two weeks at a time and, in general, not end well.

But this particular night was memorable. In routing my tour, my agent presented me with an interesting offer: a high school prom show in the middle of Indiana. Emmet, Indiana, exactly. I stood outside the school that warm June evening, sizing up the senior class as its members exited the school bus single file, having just returned from church as a group before the start of their prom. The principal, "Dr. Henry Nixon," a big corn-fed jock, sauntered over to me and said, "Now, don't be a wiseacre up there tonight."

Things got fuzzy. Church before a prom? Orderly high school seniors? Telling a comedian not to be a "wiseacre"? My buttons were being pushed.

I'm sure that, looking at me, Dr. Henry expected a high level of compliance. I do not appear to be an angry, rebellious person. I wear V-neck sweaters and khakis. My manners are above average (although the average is pretty low), and I am small. But once the buttons are pushed, this other guy emerges, and he is not compliant, rational, or aware that he is five foot eight.

The big "Catholic shame button" had been installed in me as a child on Wednesday nights during religious education classes in the homes of humorless do-gooders who would torture my friends and me. On Sundays, my mother dragged my brother, sister, and me to the eleven-thirty Mass at Transfiguration church, to which we usually arrived around eleven forty-five. Whichever pink-faced Irish Mick family was kind enough to make room for us in their pew would be subjected to three squirming, giggling children being threatened by a tiny woman with a mild hangover. Prayers and songs were mumbled until the second collection came around, at which point my mother would belt out that week's hymn with the passion of Mahalia Jackson. This allowed her to conveniently avoid the cash basket on a stick being waved in front of her by the "Worker Catholic" anointed to shake down the congregation each week.

Though I received mixed messages from my parents about church, as a child, I was a true believer. I liked Jesus, still do, so finding out in high school that the Bible was a work of fiction outraged and confused me. Since then, I've grown to look upon religious people with a wary eye, and this Emmet senior class was a fucking eyeful. Although this was a different mutation of religion—Bible Belt peer pressure versus the shame-based East Coast model I'd grown up ingesting—the results were equally toxic. A prom night kicked off by a field trip to church was missing the whole point of being a teenager.

Here is just one litter of my cousins as they gather for a drunken knife fight.

Raised by Irish parents from the Bronx, my culture was about short fuses, long grudges, and zero tolerance for giving in. The Irish gene pool is shallow and contains worse DNA than a *CSI* sperm bank: alcoholism, a psychotic temper, pasty skin accented only by freckles, melanoma, and spider veins. Physically this gruesome, the Irish had to develop a lot of charm and character just to survive. Random bursts of anger from adults seemed fine to me as a child because it was made up for by their incredible sense of humor and fun. I've always had a deep love-hate relationship with my 100 percent Irish genes.

You will not find a better party than one of my family's holidays. The evening will end listening to my relatives sing songs about fighting, and your stomach will hurt not just from a lack of any decent food but from laughing hysterically all night. You can then consider *any one* of my cousins, aunts, or uncles a dear friend for life, like it or not.

The Irish sense of humor is a reaction to living under an oppressive British occupation, brightened up by the even more repressive Catholic Church, which informed us that upon birth we are guilty of "original sin" (which is like being put on probation while punching in on your first day at a new job). All of this resulted in a people as deeply mistrustful of authority as they are proud of their dysfunction.

But these Indiana kids had no pride, no courage, no clue who they really were. Ask someone from that part of the country his or her heritage, and you're likely to hear a response like, "I think I'm an eighth Danish, half German, a quarter Norwegian, and my great-aunt was a midget." It's like the people from the coldest parts of Europe all had sex with one another and then headed off to the Osarks to birth their frozen genes in a similar climate.

Where I grew up, you were Irish, or Italian, or Colombian, or Cuban, or black, but there were no fucking fractions. Somehow those fractions annoyed me. I'm not racist against any one race; it's just that as a New Yorker, it only seemed fair that you actually *were* one.

What these dolts were missing was the joy of the rebellion. In case you missed *Dazed and Confused* or any of the *American Pie* movies, prom night is when you shed your virginity, vomit, and stay out all night. With graduation a month off, it is a final uprising against the guardian that will soon cease to be. A poignant moment to feel the daring and excitement of behaving badly, knowing underneath lies the safety net of being old enough and wise enough to keep out of any real harm.

My prom night was along those lines except for the sex part. Ten years ago, I'd invited Barbara Bennedeto to be my prom date. She was not my girlfriend, but a friend who happened to be beautiful and very cool. She agreed to go with me because we were good friends, and because I promised to secure copious amounts of cocaine. Ditching the prom dinner early, we headed to Manhattan and went to Danceteria, a huge disco that had five floors of dancing and the added luxury of admitting kids of all ages as long as they had a twenty for the Guido Neanderthal guarding the door. To give a sense of the times, on the way out of the club, I realized I'd lost one of my packets of coke. I desperately asked the bartender if he had seen it. He checked with the other bartenders, and he then discreetly slipped it back into my hands, no questions asked. I remember thinking that this was "one of the greatest nights of my life." In reality, the bartenders rightly assumed that high school kids from the suburbs get shitty coke.

Another reason that this Indiana event confused me was because it shat upon my image of what the Midwest is supposed to be. This is the real America! Where were the cool guys smoking Camels and racing cars? I

My prom night: Two guys dying to get laid, two girls who know it ain't gonna happen. Because of my looks, my publisher insisted on the blindfolds.

thought *all* Americans saw themselves as rebels. Revolution is America's creation myth. It is our MO. We justify our mundane lives by fantasizing that we are doing it our own way. Whether it's a housewife who secretly watches porn, or a lawyer who won't wear ties and smokes pot, we all quietly but defiantly play out some perversion of what is expected of us.

Had these kids missed the news? I watched a president resign amid a scandal and witnessed organized movements fight for everything from civil rights to women's rights and challenge everything from sexual harassment to war. Rebellion was back, and this was our time! Maybe it wasn't these kids' time. They reminded me more of corny 1950s America, when everyone played a lot of baseball and cried while watching fireworks.

"Don't be a wiseacre?" I said. "I'm a comedian. You hired me. Why not hire a juggler and tell him not to throw anything around?" How could Dr. Henry have known that my parents encouraged their kids to challenge anybody in charge? (Except, of course, when my parents themselves were in charge; I will get into this minor strategic error later in the book.)

The encouragement to disrespect authority was not always explicit with my parents, but in watching them, it was hard to miss. Over the years, I watched my dad park his Lincoln Town Car in front of fire hydrants and slip maître d's money to get a good table without a reservation. After dinner, the car ride home was like a video game: the Vodka Grand Prix. Pedestrians lucky enough to get out of his way saw three children's faces pressed up against the rear window much like Edvard Munch's painting *The Scream*.

My mother snuck us onto subways and into movie theaters at the under-six-years-old rate long after we started sporting chin whiskers, and she never missed a chance to make fun of people who followed the rules. I got the message loud and clear.

One of my parents' proudest moments happened on a frigid Sunday afternoon at a New York Giants football game. They turned around from their freezing *outdoor* seats to see that their ten-year-old son had snuck inside a glassed-in VIP box directly behind them and was sipping hot chocolate with his coat off. They beamed like I had just won a spelling bee. It's not that we broke the rules; we just lived by different ones.

Back on this night in Indiana, I felt like I owed it to these kids to shake them and tell them how things are supposed to be: that at this moment in your lives, you are meant to express anger and do many drugs. You are teenagers and, accordingly, owe yourselves a night where you break out of the womb of small-town polite society. These kids were brainwashed. Most of them had made pledges to stay virgins until marriage. They had said no to drugs, which made it hard to understand how they managed to listen to Bob Seger and Huey Lewis. I was trying to save them!

So I did the show, and I felt very much like Prometheus delivering the forbidden fire to the mortals. I brought the spirit of everything I saw lacking in their upbringing onto the stage that night, and the Emmet Indiana High School class of 1995 reached into their corn-fed hearts and gave me a standing ovation.

Was I a wiseacre? I'm not really sure. I had never heard the word before, and had just assumed it was some kind of farming term. The letter my agent received from the principal, however, did not reflect the positive feeling I had experienced.

When I first read it, I was angry. Dr. Henry really pissed me off. He was clearly just covering his ass. Parents sent him letters, so now he had to send

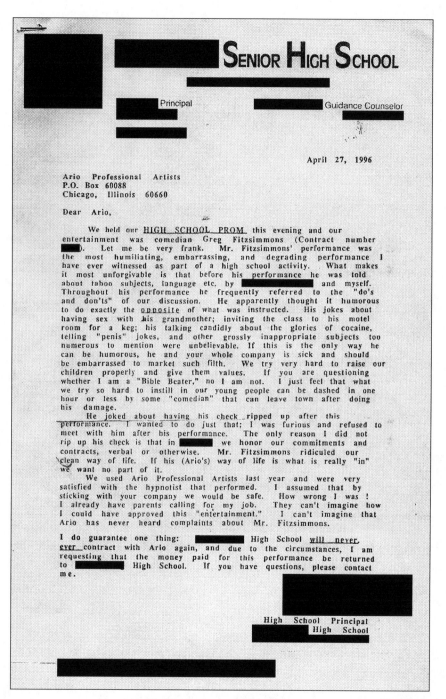

Principal   Guidance Counselor

April 27, 1996

Ario Professional Artists
P.O. Box 60088
Chicago, Illinois 60660

Dear Ario,

    We held our HIGH SCHOOL PROM this evening and our entertainment was comedian Greg Fitzsimmons (Contract number ▓▓). Let me be very frank. Mr. Fitzsimmons' performance was the most humiliating, embarrassing, and degrading performance I have ever witnessed as part of a high school activity. What makes it most unforgivable is that before his performance he was told about taboo subjects, language etc. by ▓▓▓▓▓▓▓▓ and myself. Throughout his performance he frequently referred to the "do's and don'ts" of our discussion. He apparently thought it humorous to do exactly the opposite of what was instructed. His jokes about having sex with his grandmother; inviting the class to his motel room for a keg; his talking candidly about the glories of cocaine, telling "penis" jokes, and other grossly inappropriate subjects too numerous to mention were unbelievable. If this is the only way he can be humorous, he and your whole company is sick and should be embarrassed to market such filth. We try very hard to raise our children properly and give them values. If you are questioning whether I am a "Bible Beater," no I am not. I just feel that what we try so hard to instill in our young people can be dashed in one hour or less by some "comedian" that can leave town after doing his damage.

    He joked about having his check ripped up after this performance. I wanted to do just that; I was furious and refused to meet with him after his performance. The only reason I did not rip up his check is that in ▓▓▓▓▓▓ we honor our commitments and contracts, verbal or otherwise. Mr. Fitzsimmons ridiculed our clean way of life. If his (Ario's) way of life is what is really "in" we want no part of it.

    We used Ario Professional Artists last year and were very satisfied with the hypnotist that performed. I assumed that by sticking with your company we would be safe. How wrong I was! I already have parents calling for my job. They can't imagine how I could have approved this "entertainment." I can't imagine that Ario has never heard complaints about Mr. Fitzsimmons.

I do guarantee one thing: ▓▓▓▓▓▓ High School will never, ever contract with Ario again, and due to the circumstances, I am requesting that the money paid for this performance be returned to ▓▓▓▓▓▓ High School. If you have questions, please contact me.

High School Principal
High School

The lemon that I made a lot of lemonade with.

my agent a letter, and so on and so forth. This letter reminded me of how many letters I'd gotten in my life and how bad they always made me feel when I first read them.

> I just feel that what we try so hard to instill in our young people can be dashed in one hour or less by some "comedian" that can leave town after doing his damage.

Really? If I can tell jokes for one hour and destroy the whole fabric of your community, it seems like maybe you should have created more durable fabric. Give me a break; it's not like I got them to dance or do anything truly evil!

> Mr. Fitzsimmons ridiculed our clean way of life. If his (Ario's) way of life is what is really "in" we want no part of it.

You know you're tragically uncool when you have to put quotation marks around the word *in*. Like, without the quotes, the town elders might accuse Dr. Henry of becoming hip and run him out of town.

> We used Ario Professional Artists last year and were very satisfied with the hypnotist that performed.

Naturally, a hypnotist is much more in line with Emmet's teaching methods. If I were a hypnotist, believe me, I could have done a lot more damage that night than I did. For the rest of his life, every time Dr. Henry heard me clap my hands, he would have started jacking off like a teenaged baboon.

But Dr. Henry had booked an actual comedian. He misunderstood our relationship from the get-go. He pays me, I make fun of him and his school, and then I leave (with a check).

Comedy is counterculture, and it has become my way of fighting back in life. I was raised with guilt, but comedy turned out to be my way of taking back that power. Dr. Henry struck a raw nerve in me, and I became a small, angry child again.

Like most boys, my first and most powerful authority figure was my father. Early on, I began stuffing down the anger I felt from my inability to fight back against my dad. Despite his ability to light up a room with his personality, his moods swung as wildly as Darryl Strawberry on a coke binge. At six foot one, his rage was absolutely crushing when it fell upon you, and there was no outlet for my humiliation. As I got older, I shifted the focus of this anger toward teachers, police officers, selfish automobile drivers, and even God. (He's the only one who didn't hit me for it, by the way.)

After an unpromising first quarter of my life, I found a place where I could channel all of my hate and rage in a productive manner: drunken, smoke-filled stand-up-comedy clubs. Rather than taking on the world at large, I could spew my anger at paying patrons who only encouraged the immature and self-destructive behavior.

In my pathetic nascence as a comedian, I allowed the audience to become the authority figure. Their role, like a parent, or a boss, was to either accept or reject me. Later on, the drive to be a good comedian convinced me to stop drinking and redefine my relationship with the crowd. I soon learned to take that power away from them. (Is it corny to say that this is the same relationship I have with my father? If so, you may want to skip over chapter 8, which could read to some like a pathetic Billy Crystal one-man show.) I made the audience see me as the one in charge, and if they did not accept their subordination, I punished them like bitches. Learning to control rowdy crowds night after night changed how I felt about myself to the core. I especially enjoyed the dumb jock who'd bench-pressed himself into believing he had a future. Following his heckle, a one-hundred-and-fifty-pound nothing redefined his life for him in front of a crowd of his friends. The microphone in my hand let me turn the tables on a life I'd felt bullied by up until then.

For comedians, breaking the rules is win-win. In success, we are heroes of the downtrodden; the ballsy laugh-in-the-face-of-life alcoholic perverts that other people wish they could be more like. In our failure, we are a morality tale; audience members laugh at our bad judgment and feel better about their own, more conventional lives. Society's definition of what is acceptable or inappropriate often follows the lead of what comedians get away with (or don't).

During my first appearance on *The Howard Stern Show,* Howard's long-time producer, Gary Dell'Abate, aka "Baba Booey," gave me advice that I would never forget. He told me that when I was in the studio, I should never deflect and just tell the truth. I remind myself of that every time I go back on the show. Now, rather than attach shame to embarrassing incidents, I broadcast the details on national radio, television, and stages throughout the country. My wife really wants to thank you, Gary.

In my ongoing struggle to make sense of my life, I received a helping hand in an unlikely place this past summer: my Aunt Jo's basement in the Bronx. Amidst the broken space heaters, shredded extension cords, and other fire hazards we'll all hear about on the six o'clock news someday, I learned some things I will never forget:

1. Collector's edition *Mad* magazines from the 1970s lose all their value after a crazy aunt has spread them on the floor while varnishing a table.
2. Aunt Jo has a sizable collection of used Styrofoam human organ–transport boxes from her nursing days. No, I did not look inside them.
3. My mother saved every bad report and complaint about me that she ever received. Every one.

I was now staring at a stack of my own hate mail from over twenty years ago. It felt almost grotesque, like standing on a mirror and staring at your own taint strip (from what I hear . . .). A normal parent would hide or destroy any evidence so clearly illustrating her child's failures. My mom, however, preserved each one in its original envelope like a trophy case, ensuring that, someday, I would be reminded of how much of a pain in the ass I really was.

Reading the letters, I began to understand myself more and more. They told the story of how I was bred to blindly challenge anyone, anytime, over anything. The letters pulled back the curtain of my now bourgeois life and reminded me who I really was but was now running away from. This box of letters reached out and tore the shoulder off my button-down Gap shirt, revealing a sunburnt and freckled shoulder; a tattoo of the Fighting Irish leprechaun pathetically challenging the world to a fistfight. It was in my DNA.

I cannot suppress it, and I cannot keep it from my children. I can only try to warn them of their fates.

At forty-four, I may seem young to write a memoir, but I have not exactly been sitting on my ass this whole time. Have you got a problem with that? Good, because I'm going to write another one after this one. How about that, fuck-face?

Memoirs have become the lowest form of writing, which is what drew me to the genre. It is soft and forgiving, like the enabling wife of an alcoholic. Readers will suspend their disbelief over outrageous claims just as long as the narrator is charming. The Irish have contributed generously to this form because of our gift for romanticizing and embellishing.

Although I am 100 percent Irish, 110 percent lazy, and very fond of exaggeration, I will discipline myself to writing "good honest sentences," as Hemingway instructed. As such, I am issuing a challenge to my dear reader: prove me wrong. In any instance, if you think I have stretched the truth or am full of shit, go to DearMrsFitzsimmons.com and call me on it. I will respond and tell you what a hateful piece of shit you are and why. Or I'll cop to having lost my grip on my attempt at the nonfiction version of a memoir.

James Joyce's *A Portrait of the Artist as a Young Man* set the memoir bar extremely high; it's been all downhill from there. The McCourt brothers wrote good books that were painfully truthful, but Frank suffered the wrath of the citizens of Kilkenny, who wished to be thought of in a better (less honest) light than they'd been portrayed. Typical fucking Irish.

Then came Oprah. Her book club lowered the bar on memoirs forever. I am fairly certain that I'm barred from the OBC which is fine with me because I don't rely on television shows for tips on which books to read. (That being said, I am set to promote this book on any show that will have me.) First, the Big O hoisted James Frey onto the country with his tell-all *A Million Little Pieces* (and by "all" he apparently meant "all the things he could fabricate to make his boring life seem interesting"). Then she took us to new depths with Herman Rosenblat's Holocaust memoir about being imprisoned in the Buchenwald concentration camp while a girl from the outside would pass him food through the fence. Years later they accidentally met and married. Winfrey had him on her show twice and called the story "the single greatest love story, in twenty-two years of doing this show, we've ever told on the air." When she found out he had made it up, I could swear that when she went to commercial she muttered, "that lying Jew."

Naomi Campbell admitted in an interview recently that she had not even *read* her ghostwritten autobiography. Lucky her.

Therefore, I literally open my book to you and invite your scrutiny. Maybe you beat me up in fourth-grade and demand your assault be put on the record. Perhaps you are an ex-girlfriend wishing to flesh out the chapter on my sexual skill set. More likely, you are one of the hundreds of thousands of people who ingested fried onion rings and a two-drink minimum while I made cracks about how gay your shirt was. If I bombed, yet failed to detail it in my journal, go to the site, write it down, then just sit and wait. I've got nothing to hide except that one thing, but hopefully that won't come up on the website. I'd appreciate you not putting it up there.

If I seem defensive about the contents of this book, it is probably because, despite my violent tendencies, I am a small, friendly forty-four-year-old man with a receding hairline and a loving family. You would not think to look at me that I have done the things I have done. I don't wear a leather jacket, I have no tattoos, and I drive a Volkswagen Passat. For this reason, I have included the letters, behavioral reports, and arrest documents to back up the stories in these pages. I am showing my work. Unlike James Frey.

For some reason, I have always tested the limits and taken things to the edge of what is allowed. I don't step too far over the line, but I don't trust anything that's not right up against it. This behavior has, and still does, make my life far more difficult than if I had just shut up and done what I was told. I am the better for it in most ways, but, quite frankly, I'm fucking tired and look forward to a life with less testosterone, fewer things to prove, and less boundary testing.

Throughout my life, I have felt myself fighting a seemingly invincible power. Looking back now, I see that often I gave this power to people in authority. I now have the insight to see that I was creating the fight myself. In other words, very often I was being an asshole.

The first dusty letter I exhumed from the A&P milk crate (clearly marked "It is unlawful to keep this crate") brought me back to 1980 and the tenth

```
                    RYE COUNTRY DAY SCHOOL
                       RYE, NEW YORK


                       D E T E N T I O N

Student's Name  Greg Fitzsimmons    Grade    10
Reason for Detention  I was teaching proportions and
said, "This is the 1st position, 2nd position, etc."
Greg then called out, "Are there any other
positions? Is there "69"?"
Faculty Member  Peter Solomon    Date  2/17
Detention Assignment  Saturday  2/20/82
Detention Date


_____          _____
    Student Signature              Detention Supervisor
Advisor  _____
                                 _____
                                     Date Served
```

My parents were horrified that I knew about the 69 position. I was more horrified that they also knew.

grade. It was that awkward stage for an Irish boy where the relief of finally sprouting a few pubic hairs is quickly replaced by the horror that they are orange.

My father had just finished "eating" (my mother is not a very good "cook"), when my mother slid an envelope across our Formica dinner table. Consuming his own body weight in red meat and booze each week had taken its toll, yet to me, my dad seemed indestructible. As he pushed his chair back with his two-hundred-pound frame, he lit his fiftieth Viceroy cigarette of the day. (I believe the pack came with a skull and crossbones on the side. Eventually the skull and crossbones sued Viceroy for defamation.) That night, his mood seemed not good. Opening the envelope with his bloodied steak knife, he expelled two to three metric quarts of smoke from his nostrils as if doing so were not only natural but also really good for you. He then read the letter aloud.

15

As my father exited the kitchen, the hallway floorboards whined under his steps. The belts hung in his closet, and I heard him select one with the same care of Tiger Woods selecting an iron at the U.S. Open. With no creamed corn left to spear with my fork, I tried in vain to make eye contact with a family member. My older brother, Bobby, cracked his knuckles and went back to gnawing his anemic pork chop, safe in knowing that tonight it was not about him. My little sister, Deirdre, nervously lobbed out an attempt at small talk, but it fell to the floor unheard. Finally, my mother stood up and left the room. It felt like the town square clearing out before the gunfight in *High Noon*. I was the guy who knows he's about to lose the gunfight but has to show up anyway because there's nowhere else to go because he lives in this shitty one-horse town and he's fourteen and the better gunfighter owned the house and had anger issues. (I may have lost the metaphor back there.)

Suddenly, from the other side of the house, came the purifying sound of laughter. It signaled a reprieve: all was safe now, and I would live to see another day.

"Pass the milk," my brother said, smiling.

Deirdre covered her mouth and giggled.

It was like that. You never knew the reaction a letter would solicit. You had to factor in my parents' mood, how long ago the last letter had been written, but most important, how funny the letter was. Funny went a long way, yet the teachers appealing for change through these missives were unaware of how their attempts could blow up in their faces. In the context of our family's absurd culture, most notes produced howls of laughter, which only encouraged more disrespectful behavior.

In keeping with this tradition, I began reading the Indiana prom letter on stages all over the country. Not only did my anger begin to recede, but people howled uncontrollably at the uptight principal and his sad little worldview. I included the letter in a stand-up special I did for Comedy Central, then mailed a videotaped copy of it to Dr. Henry Nixon back in Indiana. I never heard back from him. Perhaps he does not yet have a VCR, but, more likely, he fears the obvious: that he has become like a father figure to me. Dr. Henry, if you are reading this, *please call me!*

Kick Me, I'm Irish

Their wailing cries shook the very heavens,
and my four green fields ran red with their blood, said she.

—Traditional Irish ballad

Patricia Marie Judith McCarthy Fitzsimmons did not receive a very good education—not at home and not in Catholic school. Fifteen years of abuse from the nuns at St. Benedict's Catholic School left her feeling below average. Most of the holy sisters had signed up for the "I'm a lesbian in the 1950s, so hide me in a nunnery" program. Instead they were directed to their worst nightmare: teaching pasty-faced wiseass Irish and Italian kids (who became their human punching bags).

From what I understand, both of my parents got into a lot of trouble in their Catholic schools. The worst part was that if they told their folks that the nuns had slapped them around, their parents would beat them again. It's the classic Irish "double beating."

What endured was a reflexive disrespect for authority. While my mom is the first person to stop and help a homeless person, a cashier undercharging her was seen as a stroke of good luck. Any rule that meant extra effort or less fun for her kids was stamped "irrelevant." Height lines for a roller coaster were for wimpy kids, not us. This attitude never affected her love of people and joy for life. She has always left an indelible mark on everyone she meets. When my mother flies, she takes a long cab ride to the airport.

17

Without exception, whether the driver is fat or elderly, black or Hispanic—it doesn't matter—when he arrives at the airport, he gets out of the cab, pulls my mom's bag from the trunk, and then gives her a hug. Because she listened to him for the entire ride; she laughed with him and cared about what he told her. But if he undercharged her, she didn't say shit about it.

My mother was the youngest of six kids (one died young from tuberculosis). Both her parents immigrated here as teenagers by themselves before meeting at a church dance in the Bronx. Pop worked for Con Edison (the electric company) for forty years and, after retiring, worked part-time at Baskin-Robbins so he could swipe ice cream for the grandkids. He'd cheerfully deliver pints of bright green chocolate chip mint during every visit, and his fridge was packed with the stuff.

Pop had also pocketed washers from work, which doubled as slugs for pay phones. The ruse went on well into my mother's adulthood, and was finally busted by a cop when my mother, with me in a stroller, told him that her dime was stuck in the payphone. When he pushed on the coin return, the washer came tumbling out, and the gig was up.

My maternal grandmother seems to have displayed little of Pop's spirit. While he sat at the dinner table reciting limericks he learned as a boy back in County Kerry, Ireland, she holed up alone in the kitchen, telling her kids, "It's less work for me to just do it on my own." My hunch is that Grandma was more interested in spending quality time with a little Bushmills whiskey than with five hungry children. She was the classic Irish matriarch, and although her kids feared her, they respected her intelligence. They knew that she was capable of more in life, but college and a career were never in the cards for an immigrant woman with a life of financial struggle and annoying children.

My mother's father, Francis, was a real character. If he liked you, he'd call you "one of the best." His real name was Florence, and back in County Kerry, he ran messages for the Irish Republican Army until his family had enough money to ship him to America when he was sixteen. They shipped over each of his eleven siblings, one by one. (It sounds desperate, but *you* try living in a two-room house with one bathroom on a diet of turnips and black beer.)

This note, found in my mom's closet, seems to have been written under duress. If she had cut out the letters from magazines, like a ransom note, it wouldn't have had more feeling.

When Florence learned that his future son-in-law was a radio announcer, he said, "Well, he may come home hungry, but he'll never come home tired." Florence switched his name to Frank after several years of having to fight the "Eye-talians" who teased him about it. At the age of seventy, he defiantly switched his name back to Florence. His grandkids immediately beat the shit out of him because it was a stupid name. He's lucky I even put it in the book.

My father teased my mother her whole life about the fact that, when he met her, Pop was still cutting up her meat at dinner. Young Patricia got a hard time from her siblings for getting treated special as the youngest, but

No, Pop was not
in the Irish mob.
As far as you know.

Mom's family before she came along. Their faces reflect the embarrassment of an Irish family with so few offspring.

the child who got the royal treatment was her older brother, Francis. At age eleven, Francis and the rest of the kids had already logged over twenty thousand hours of kneeling, rising, bowing, crossing, and confessing at St. Benedict's Roman Catholic Church, where Masses were said in Latin. One evening, in a rare moment of quiet on Edison Avenue, a vision of the Holy Mother appeared before Francis. Bingo! From that point forward, he was treated like a saint. He excelled at school, and led a very full and rich life, raising six children of his own. They all go to the same church and the same country club and have mass-produced beautiful freckle-faced children of their own. Francis passed away in 2010, and it was like our family had lost the chairman of the board. He was beloved for his kindness, charity, and joy. I asked my mother if he really saw the Holy Mother. Without hesitation she said to me, "Yes." Not only was Francis an incredibly good man, he was a genius.

My mother grew up in the shadow of all of her older siblings. Dolores is the closest in age and a world-class ballbuster. The only person she teases more than my mother is herself. She proudly acknowledges being the worst cook in America (the only nominees are Irish) and cemented the title this past Easter when she prepared the meal for my family. She presented a lime cake, the recipe of which she'd clipped from a magazine. It weighed nine pounds and refused to allow the knife in my hand to penetrate. We were dying of laughter as I finally chipped out petrified slices and served them to my now crying family. Using my full body weight to push the fork through my piece of limestone cake, the utensil snapped in half, and the hysteria went on for no less than fifteen minutes.

Mom's oldest sister, Peggy, was pretty tough as well. She moved out to Long Island with my uncle Paul and pumped out six little leprechauns: Kevin, Gerard, Marypat, Brian, Jeanine, and Danny. Sounds like the starting lineup for an Alcoholics Anonymous hockey team.

The neighbor had a vicious German shepherd. This greatly upset Peggy, having been attacked by a dog as a child. My mom told me conspiratorially one day that the dog "ate some special Gaines-Burgers" and wasn't around anymore. There's a sly pride in my mother's telling of the story. It's how her family took care of things.

I think the fear of Grandma brought my mom's siblings closer to one another. Despite this closeness, however, it was always clear that my mom was going to live a life different from the others'. When she met my dad, that suspicion became a certainty.

I think one of the things that made my mother fall hard for my dad was the way he treated her mother. He charmed my grandmother with great success, always dressing up when he came over as my parents first started dating. Also, Grandma did not intimidate him. He once found a glass of whiskey behind the toaster and asked if it was hers. She hissed, "Heavens, no! It must be left from the last dinner party." My father held up the glass and complimented Grandma on having the longest-lasting ice cubes in the Bronx. Anybody else would have gotten a smack. My father got a laugh and a wave of her hand.

If you want a long marriage, then marry an Irish person. It may not be a good marriage, but it will last forever. We don't cheat, because there is too much guilt, and besides, no one will fuck us.

Seeing an old Irish couple walking arm in arm after forty years together, don't be fooled. It may seem romantic, but it's really just survival. He's got a bad knee, she needs hip surgery; it's pretty much the only way they can walk upright. At this point, they're just drunkenly cursing, and trying to make it to the finish line.

The pride in being Irish is as unparalleled as it is unwarranted. During my wife's first pregnancy, the OB-GYN placed a stickpin with Erin's name on it and our son's due date on a wall calendar. Other doctors in the practice shared the calendar, and I pointed out that there was a cluster of pins right around Christmas. On closer inspection, I saw that the mothers' names showed a pattern: O'Brien, McCarthy, Ryan, Fitzpatrick. A mass of newborns were expected on or near December 25, just like Jesus. I got goose bumps. It seems ridiculous, but there are sometimes signs that the Irish are truly special, if not divine. I pointed out the pattern to my wife and her doctor with restrained mystical pride. The doctor callously dismissed my findings with four cold (and borderline racist) words: Saint Patrick's Day babies. Christmas is nine months after Saint Patrick's Day. So there's nothing

To the untrained eye, this looks like Christmas. In fact, this is me and Mom on Saint Patrick's Day, circa 1983. This had traditionally been the day before we would take down the tree.

"divine" about it. It's just the result of drunken unprotected make-up sex after a slap fight at the Blarney Stone that day.

Roughly six months after my parents' impromptu wedding in Ireland, my mother rested comfortably in the maternity ward after giving birth to my older brother, Bobby. Shortly thereafter, my grandmother entered the room, lunged at her daughter, and, enraged over the scandal, tried to strangle her. My grandfather and father had to pull this lunatic off of my mother.

Meeting my father marked an exciting adventure that, although it took my mother less than twenty miles away, swept her into a completely different world. And she was glad to be gone from the old one.

Poppa Played the Rolling Stones (and Sinatra)

"What are you rebelling against, Johnny?"

"Whaddya got?"

—Marlon Brando in *The Wild One*

My parents met at a house party out in Hampton Bays, Long Island. My mom and her friends rented out a place that became known as "our house" because of all the freeloaders on the couch, floor, and backyard on any given weekend. My mom was hot stuff and once even won the Miss Cresthaven beauty contest in Queens one year. The tiara would sit hiding on the top shelf of our parents' closet our whole lives. It was never taken down, but we'd get glimpses of it and see that Mom had had another life once.

If my dad was drawn to my mother's beauty and sense of humor, she was drawn to his big personality. To this day, I meet guys who grew up with him who have stories about what a wiseass he was. He and his boys ran in basketball games in Washington Heights and other nearby neighborhoods, and Dad seems to have made legions of friends in every borough of New York.

My father pursued my mom throughout the summer, and by the fall, they were together. His charm and self-deprecating humor made him hard to resist, but it was the fact that he had a vision for his future and a lot of drive that sealed the deal. All of these traits would combine to eventually

If you know what I had to do for this fucking crown, you'd shit!

She seems to have failed to capture the eye of this judge, who is instead gazing out at the alter-boy weightlifting competition in the yard.

make him one of the most familiar voices on radio in New York, the city in which he grew up.

Bob Fitzsimmons and his brother, Jimmy, were born in Queens before moving up to the Bronx (the nice section called Riverdale) when their dad was promoted to comptroller at McGraw-Hill Publishing. Here's the thing about my dad: when he was fifteen, his father died, and within a few years of that, his mother passed as well. My dad used the money left to him to attend college, while Jimmy drank his inheritance away. This left my dad to look after his abusive older brother for the rest of his life. Jimmy was a skid-row alcoholic, but my dad always made sure there was a roof over his head by paying his rent on the Bowery. That is about all I know about my dad's childhood.

I cannot remember my father ever talking to me about his early life. Not once. I don't know a single Fitzsimmons relative, and few pictures exist. Since Uncle Jimmy and my dad both died long before I decided to write this

One picture I did find: Dad's prom night. Camel, no filter? Check. Bottle of whiskey? Check. Fat chick? Bingo.

book, I have almost no information about his boyhood. As it stands now, my son, Owen, is the only person who will carry on the Fitzsimmons name. And he can barely spell it.

After completing a two-year degree at Boston University, my dad returned to New York, where he spent a few years working at Patricia Murphy's Candlelight Restaurant, a renowned eatery in Yonkers. Upon completion of basic training in Fort Drum, New York, my dad headed to the West Coast to avoid military service. He wasn't a draft dodger; that's cowardly. But he also wasn't the kind of guy who was going to be able to take orders. The one or two stories he told about this time usually ended in him having to push a wheelbarrow for hours as punishment.

Relocating to California simply made assigning him to duty more cumbersome for the army. In the meantime, he worked as an usher for a kids' TV show, living within a couple of miles of Venice Beach, where I'm now living forty years later.

In 1962, a friend of his family named Bobby Fasselt brought my dad back to New York to work as an intern on the legendary *Klavan and Finch* morning radio show on WNEW-AM. For about fifteen years *Klavan and Finch* stayed at the top of the ratings with comedy sketches and characters. They needed a traffic guy, Trevor Traffic, and although my father had no experience in this area, he got the job because he was not Jewish. At first he was offended that he had been hired by an anti-Semitic station manager, but he learned that the previous traffic guy took off all of the Jewish holidays, and the manager knew that a good Catholic boy would work on Easter Sunday if it meant a paycheck.

This entrée allowed my father to learn from and interact with two of the most respected guys in radio. At a different job, coming in late and hung over might have cost him his job, but his older, less wild bosses began counting on my father's partying stories. Having a boss who found his misbehavior amusing became a prerequisite for employment for my dad, and later for me as well. But his was ultimately an assistant job, and he would need to prove himself in smaller markets before ever rising up in the New York market. It was around this time that my parents got serious with each other and embraced the 1960s like only a disc jockey couple could.

Even black people on *Soul Train* thought these outfits were a little over the top.

Those outfits soon led to a pregnancy. My mother was traveling in Europe when she found out and my dad traveled over to Ireland so they could have a romantic wedding ceremony in the town my dad's family was from. Not far behind were Mom's parents, neither of whom had been back to the old sod since crossing the pond many years before. It was apparently an amazing time.

My parents' wedding. The other two people in the photo finally got married last year in Massachusetts.

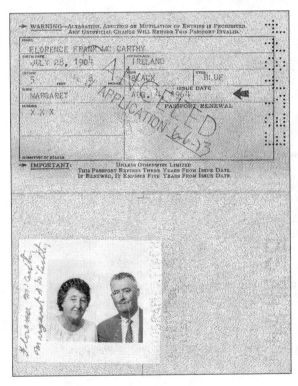

My grandparents' 1964 passport. With the purchase of this book, you are allowed to steal their identities. (Hopefully, you'll have better luck with them than they did.)

For my dad, judging beauty contests was a great way of promoting his radio career. That's actually what he told my mother.

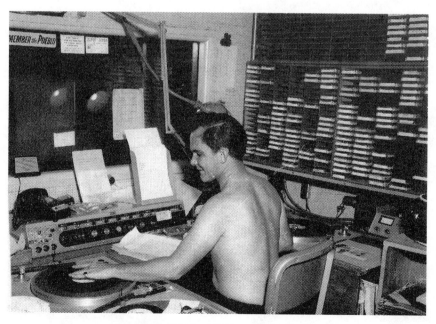

My dad, the Matthew McConaughey of radio.

They returned from the wedding and moved into what had been my father's boyhood home in the Riverdale section of the Bronx. He landed his own radio show in Rockland County, New York, about an hour north of the city, working out of a trailer at WRKL. A sign warned people not to flush the toilet while a show was going on. My mother would send my father to work with egg cartons to use as soundproofing. She believed in him and was as invested in his dream as he was. He spent time learning to act in community theater and exploring show business.

Thirteen months after my brother Bobby's birth, I came screaming into the picture—literally. As an infant, I had a blocked intestine and apparently cried nonstop for close to two months. Between doing morning radio and dealing with two boys a year apart, my father finally lost it. My mother walked into the apartment one day to find him dangling me, at about eight months old, out the window by my ankles. This was years before Michael Jackson made it cool. (Note to self: contact Blanket Jackson about a recovery support group.)

Dad uprooted the family to pursue his broadcasting career, which invariably meant that he had to go to Ohio for a period of time. We spent a year

We were cute. And my mom was hot. (*Awkward . . .*)

We were cute. And my dad was lucky.

in Youngstown when I was about three years old, where Dad took over the mike at WFMI. My mom describes this as the worst year of her life. This was followed by two years in Cherry Hill, New Jersey, as my father worked his way up at WPEN in Philly. While camped out in Cherry Hill, my father received mediocre offers of part-time slots in the New York radio market. My mother insisted that he wait for the real offer of a full-time job at a legitimate station before moving back to New York.

It was here that my sister, Deirdre, was born. Things seemed like they were settling down when in 1970 Dad got a job offer in Chicago; an opportunity to be in a major market with his own show. My mom said, "I will go to Chicago happily. But only after you try to get a job in New York."

Dad got up his nerve and called a guy he'd known from years back, now the station manager at WHN in New York. He asked if there were any openings at the station. The guy said, "I've been waiting for you to call." My father was offered a full-time position at WHN and we moved back to New York two weeks later. Dad was in the big leagues, where he'd started out as an intern traffic guy ten years earlier. Except now it was his show.

31

In the meantime, my parents were winging it in the parenting department. Within the span of nineteen months, they had gotten married and had two kids and were now learning on the job. My mother was still just a girl when she had my older brother. She'd never been taught how to cook, and she still lived in her parents' house when she married my dad. With my father's parents already gone, and my mother's folks burnt after twenty grandkids and counting, they were on their own.

Our home in New Jersey is my first childhood memory, thankfully. It was a green house in which I shared a room with my brother. Bobby and I are classic "Irish twins": thirteen months apart and fighting not only for friends but also for attention from our parents. After about two weeks of nightly fistfights, my parents ran out of solutions and moved me into the TV room. This didn't stop them from putting us both in the same preschool class later that year. Apparently the brawling continued.

The first bad reports my mother saved arrived at the tender age of five. My preschool teacher, Mrs. Johnson, sent letters home with veiled implications that my parents had delivered me to her with absolutely no preparation whatsoever. Either my parents had neglected me, or Mrs. Johnson was a little fuzzy on the concept of *preschool*.

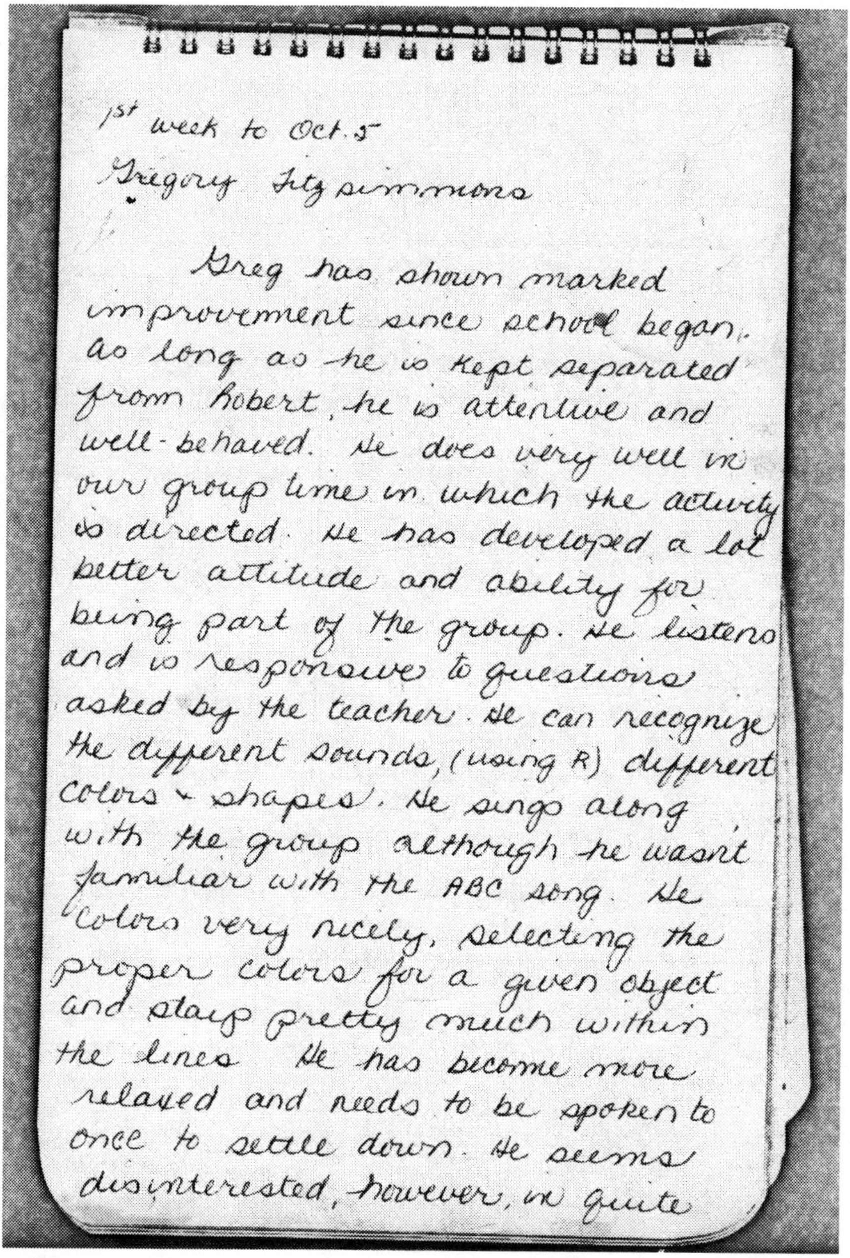

1st week to Oct. 5

Gregory Fitzsimmons

Greg has shown marked improvement since school began. As long as he is kept separated from Robert, he is attentive and well-behaved. He does very well in our group time in which the activity is directed. He has developed a lot better attitude and ability for being part of the group. He listens and is responsive to questions asked by the teacher. He can recognize the different sounds, (using R) different colors & shapes. He sings along with the group although he wasn't familiar with the ABC song. He colors very nicely, selecting the proper colors for a given object and stays pretty much within the lines. He has become more relaxed and needs to be spoken to once to settle down. He seems disinterested, however, in quite

That's right; my first "Dear Mrs. Fitzsimmons" letter!

1st week to Oct 5

Greg has shown marked improvement since school began. As long as he is kept separated from Robert... He sings along with the group although he wasn't familiar with the ABC song...

He needs improvement in word concepts (first, last, middle) and number concepts. He is not familiar with a lot of things - he didn't know what a ferris wheel was, how to wiggle, what a heel or an elbow was, what a train engine & a caboose is...

He seems disinterested, however, in quite a few of the center activities. He has only been in the Expressive Arts center once where he pasted a very nice picture using only 2 pieces of paper. He glued them on in a few seconds & then got up and left. I feel that Greg is a very independent child, not requiring contact with the teacher...

Gregory Fitzsimmons 11/24/70
Greg is very intelligent, but shy when asked to perform for a teacher...

Who the fuck drops their kid off at preschool not knowing how to wiggle?

Early Disciplinary Reports; Or,
As We Called Them, Irish Merit Badges

My overjoyed father rushed his family back to New York and purchased a home in Tarrytown that he could not afford. He later told me that he wanted to put pressure on himself by buying the house. My dad always responded well to pressure, as long as it was his own pressure, not pressure from his bosses.

The Tarrytown area is where Don Draper, the main character of the television show *Mad Men*, commutes to New York City from. On the surface, it's an idyllic suburban community. But Tarrytown also had a large General Motors plant, housing projects, and, without a doubt, the most diverse population in Westchester County. Ronald Reagan made Tarrytown famous in the early 1980s during an attack on the welfare system. He talked about a town whose median income was $60,000 a year, yet gave 60 percent of its children free school lunches. What he failed to mention was that the Rockefeller estate was on the edge of town, offsetting the existing poverty in the projects of downtown Tarrytown. The GM plant (now closed, of course) provided jobs for most of the townspeople. I can remember many summers of race riots, drug-related crime, and an inordinate number of teen deaths. Many of those involved my friends.

My family was without a doubt on the right side of the tracks. We lived up a very steep hill next to Marymount College, surrounded by acres upon

Not wanting to ruin Christmas, Mom never bought a tree taller than my father.

acres of undeveloped beauty owned by the Rockefellers. This did not soften the effects on my mother of growing up poor in the Bronx. She cut corners wherever she could while my dad spent money in the city like a mafia bigwig. Our family photo albums were filled with proof of her cheapness. Literally:

More proof that my mother was not paying for school pictures.

Back in New York, my dad's career began to flourish. He was an incredible radio personality, not because he was the smoothest (he was), or the most opinionated (he was), or the nicest (he was not). He listened. His shift was midday, from eleven to three, during which he took phone calls from his listeners, most of whom were middle-aged women. He talked about female issues like married sex, menopause, and divorce. At that time, very few people dared swim in those waters in broadcasting and he got into trouble for it. Then he got good ratings for it. My mother told me that after warnings from the radio brass, he was fired for it.

The format he developed became known as "the feminine forum." Housewives, then America's silent masses, finally had a chance to talk to someone who listened to them. They talked about loneliness and the difficulties of raising kids. At the time, this was revolutionary.

Although he was a radio guy, he quickly turned into a recognizable celebrity in the New York area because of the number of newspaper pieces about him that included photos. Throughout my young life, whether we were at a Giants game, eating at a great steak house, or just walking down

In the seventies, my dad signed more autographs at Shea Stadium than the Mets.

Fifth Avenue, there was always a familiar cry: "Hey, Fitz!" Turning around with a smile, my dad was as likely to see a radio fan as he was a buddy he had known from childhood or an acquaintance he'd helped out in the past.

He also became a household face for his many years as the New York host of The Jerry Lewis Telethon and years later as the original host of "Good Day New York". My dad's personality was a perfect fit in a city that liked to talk back: he was fast, tough, and funny. I grew up watching and learning that some rules don't apply to everyone. I saw that with the right attitude, what got one person in trouble got another one big laughs and a career.

He was an outspoken and unapologetic liberal; he had balls and could take on anyone in a debate. Later on, New York's mayor, Ed Koch, called into the show every morning, and they often battled it out. One of my dad's favorite jobs was subbing for a right-wing guy on the station named Bob Grant. Bob Grant was the original Rush Limbaugh and he was *huge* in the New York market. Grant's listeners would dial in and challenge my father. They were regularly taken apart, educated, and then hung up on. This is a technique I have had great success with just forty short years later.

As a radio broadcaster (he'd dress you down if you called him a DJ), he went through jobs pretty regularly. He spoke his mind and lost his temper when being told what to do by bosses he considered to be morons. Because of this obstinacy, there was always a lot of drama, but he always found more work, managing to go through life without anyone ever being in charge of him.

Bob Fitzsimmons didn't just talk, he also walked the liberal walk. Like my mother, he was doing charity work constantly and quietly, whether organizing a benefit for a struggling school or volunteering to emcee a dinner for a local charity. My folks' volunteerism was a seamless part of their lives. I grew up watching two people who made others laugh when they didn't have to. They were the ones who made the tollbooth collector smile with a comment about how Jersey drivers suck, or a waitress loiter to share one more quick story when they discovered they had something in common with her.

The story that I always felt summed up my dad involved an engineer he'd worked with for years named Pete Feldman. They had a volatile but productive relationship that spilled onto the air at times when my father would yell at him for making a mistake. I can remember Pete actually walking out of the studio on my father a couple of times. This was all good radio, and they formed a bond over time that outlasted several different station managers and program directors.

Pete developed cancer at a young age. He had a wife and kids, so he had to work, but the sickness made running the soundboard during my father's show very draining. The station decided it was time to let Pete go.

When my father found out, he didn't say a word about it on the air, but behind the scenes he issued an ultimatum: if Pete goes, I go. Pete was brought back to work, where my father continued to bust his cancerous balls whenever he'd make a mistake.

A few nights every month, my father would emcee a charity event, and sometimes I could tag along. Without a doubt, had he been born twenty-five years later (say, around the time I was born), he would have been a stand-up comedian. One Saturday afternoon, he dragged the whole family to a TV studio because Soupy Sales was hosting a telethon. Soupy had one of the strangest careers in the history of show business, alternating between radio shows, goofy local TV shows, and being a professional game-show panelist. This led to an odd celebrity status, and we were lucky enough to have a father who knew Soupy. We were given "all access" laminates and told that we were "VIPs." I remember learning that day that VIP stood for "very important person." And that's what we felt like when we were with my dad. He was a big deal. He knew Soupy Sales.

Once we got inside, before I knew what hit me, Brooke Shields walked into the green room. I was only fourteen years old and the mixture of her celebrity, her height, and her beauty made me feel even skinnier, frecklier, and less significant than I'd ever felt in my life. Brooke stood chitchatting in the corner with a girl who at the time was starring as Annie on Broadway. Annie had dark red hair, and somehow I remember thinking that her life had a lot of pain ahead of it. I'll have to Google her once I finish writing this book.

But Brooke was a vision. Hot off *Pretty Baby* and about to film *The Blue Lagoon,* she wore a blazer and a lot of makeup. In *Pretty Baby* she had no blazer, or any other clothes, and I had masturbated to that image so often

Get me out of here before these Irish kids rape me!

that the Catholic boy in me felt like walking over and apologizing. (Disclaimer: Body doubles were allegedly used for her nude scenes, but try telling that to a masturbating teenager.) We were lucky enough to have a photo taken with her. When we received the photo in the mail a week later, all of my fears were there for everyone to see. A statuesque, photographic beauty looming a full head above a thin, long-haired, pathetic, freckly failure.

My dad became the New York host of the annual Jerry Lewis Muscular Dystrophy telethon in 1974 and continued on for fifteen years. He would often bring our whole family on, and we'd make jokes (not about the kids, of course).

During one of those telethons, our family acquired a set of pictures that would define our lives for years to come. VIPs were treated to complimentary portraits done on the spot by a caricature artist, who may or

We were "Bob's Kids," though we didn't get competitive with "Jerry's Kids." (They did get the lion's share of the attention around the set.)

may not have been several decades beyond his prime. What better gift can one receive than a depiction of your worst traits blown up by the shaky hand of a deranged artist? And always playing a sport that you don't even really play.

Traditionally, upper-middle-class families hang handsome oil portraits of the family above the mantel. My family's version of that was three badly drawn caricatures framed and hanging at odd angles in the hallway. The depiction of me showed my bulbous head covered in freckles the size of silver dollars. You could drive a van through the gap drawn between my two front teeth. My stringy, greasy hair hung off my head like wet spaghetti. In my hand, for some illogical reason, was a small tennis racket. I don't think we ever turned the hallway light on again. It became known as "the corridor of low self-esteem."

Our home, which can only be described as an explosion of shag paisley, would forever be stuck in 1972. My parents' bedroom was covered in *orange*. Not just the walls, not just the bedspread, not just the curtains. Everything. It looked like a Cheetos factory.

This was years before the discovery of mousse or hair gel.

There were two large pieces of furniture—relics of my father's parents. The shiny black marble dressers must have weighed a ton, and they stood out from the rest of the décor in their heaviness. The drawers slid in and out with the ease of a Fleetwood Cadillac, and they were my only windows into what my dad's previous life had been like. They symbolized to me the strength and weight my dad seemed to carry at all times.

Every room in the house had shag carpeting below thick-striped wallpaper of various colors and patterns. Other walls were white stucco, applied by my mother in her effort at home improvement. I would bet my kids' college funds that the stucco had asbestos in it. The TV room looked like the headquarters for *The Mod Squad*. The green and yellow paisley curtains framed our view of the George Washington Bridge and New York City skyline on one side, and the GM plant on the other. The coup de grâce of the TV room was a round, red upholstered love seat on wheels with wooden armrests and a raised backrest. It was like an intergalactic space vehicle for Sonny and Cher. Over the years, as the chair wore out, my brother, sister, and I would pick at the foam cushions, leaving a daily blanket of stuffing on its surface.

One day, my mom decided that the red circular love seat had served us well and needed to be retired. I'm not sure what gave her that impression. Was it that the threads dangled over the surface like a bad comb-over, or that the guts no longer remained and were now replaced by springs jutting dangerously from its belly? Either way, I had a vision. My brother, sister, and I pushed the chair out the door and up the driveway, and began running behind it like we were in an Olympic luge competition. Our street sloped down to two bigger streets, all downhill at roughly 45-degree angles.

Although it was not unusual to see the Fitzsimmons kids playing out some act of familial humiliation in the street, this was a new one. Three demonic, emaciated-looking children screaming down the middle of a major street at thirty miles an hour on a red love seat. We bounced off curbs, narrowly missing oncoming vehicles, and by the end—with my brother and sister having wisely bailed out on people's lawns—I was the only one left on the chair as it toppled down an embankment into a creek. We licked our wounds and walked back up to the house, where my mother sat in the kitchen sharing coffee with a friend and laughing about what silly kids we were.

I can't imagine the fright our neighbors experienced when a Fitzsimmons kid approached their house. We were either going to vandalize something, try to play with one of their children, or, worse, sell them something. Entrepreneurialism was somehow born into us. I can remember going door-to-door trying to sell my neighbors berries we had picked off of their own bushes. They were likely poisonous. I remember going door-to-door with a wagon selling some type of medical magazine, clearly bearing the address of our neighbor, Dr. Eisner, on the front cover. I think this strange behavior, in a way, reassured my parents that we would all land on our feet financially as we grew up.

My parents played zone defense, not getting caught up in micromanaging us, but I also believe that raising children was less complicated in the early 1970s than it is now. Looking around at all of the precious parenting that goes on in Los Angeles, I would equate my parents' style more with that of sea turtles' parents. We were each pointed in the right direction, and then we scrambled for the ocean. Once old enough for school, we were walked in a panic down to the corner to meet a yellow bus. There were actually a number of yellow buses that came in quick succession. Parents then relied on the bus driver to determine which school the child appeared right for. At three o'clock, parents reconvened at the corner to collect their children, who, in theory, had just been taught in a school all day.

In Los Angeles, I spend Saturdays at kid parties, where I'm frequently interrogated about where my children are going to school and where they will go next. My dad didn't even know what grade I was in, but I am expected to be well versed on which "waiting list" my kids are on for which magnet programs in what charter school.

I get it. We all had bad childhoods, and we need to make up for it by giving our kids every chance at building self-esteem. They will need it in order to care for their neurotic parents who will have nervous breakdowns by age sixty. I went to public school in New York, and it was horrible. I got beat up, I was ill-prepared for college, and I spent most of my childhood bored out of my skull. But I never had to suffer through my parents asking me how I really felt or having me tested for a gifted-child middle school.

I am jealous when I remember my father waking up after we did. Because he was often out late at night "entertaining," the cardinal rule was not to make any noise in the morning. Instead we crept around like diamond thieves. We ate breakfast quietly, because one of the scariest things you could hear from the other side of the house was "Stop beating those goddamn bowls!"

There were, however, certain issues that my folks took very seriously. Beatings from teachers were at the top of that list.

In first grade, my teacher, Mrs. Branley, slapped me. I don't remember why. I had assumed that my teacher was allowed to hit me—like my parents, my grandparents, my aunts and uncles, and my good family friends. On hearing the news, however, my mother was irate, and she marched me back to school. She walked up to Mrs. Branley in front of a gymnasium full of parents gathered for a PTA meeting and slapped her across the face.

Mrs. Branley just looked at my mother. The other parents looked at my

Standing beside my girlfriend, "The Forehead."

mother. I looked at Mrs. Branley. I felt like saying, "See that, bitch! Keep it up, and my dad will come down here and really throw a beating on you." It was sweet. My mom took me home and we had dinner. I didn't take my eyes off of her or stop grinning the entire meal. Fucking awesome lesson in life.

If parenting was sometimes puzzling to my folks, they were very natural with marriage. They had a true romance. They found each other interesting, funny, and attractive. They had an active social life, going out to dinner at least two or three nights a week and often not returning home until three or four in the morning. They played golf together and never tired of each other's company. Because he worked at a radio station, my father had access to great tables at the best restaurants in the city, baseball games, and great seats for Frank Sinatra concerts. My mother wore fur coats and received expensive jewelry from my father on her birthday and Christmas.

My parents enjoyed having children. They laughed with us, and they were sometimes even proud of us. One of my mother's favorite stories involved a friend of mine named Richard Dama. Sometime around second grade, he and I were good buddies with four or five other boys. One of them sent out invitations to a birthday party, and I was upset to find out that Richard had not been invited. My mother called the boy's mother to find out why and then let it slip that it was because Richard was black.

My parents didn't shield us from the uglier issues in life because they felt we should be aware of them even at a young age. I thought about it for a while and then told my mother I would not be going to the party. Instead I hung out with Richard Black (my new name for him). Back then it wasn't called a play date, and back then your parents shot seventy-three photographs of their children having a black kid over to the house. I found out the following Monday that the party had sucked anyway. Who doesn't know that you need at least one black guy and one Irish guy to throw a decent bash? Morons.

The success of my father's radio show soon brought him lucrative voice-over jobs on commercials. We joined a country club in White Plains called Knollwood. It's not at all what you might picture when you think of a country club in Westchester. The people were very down to earth and cool. They were working-class Italian and Irish families who'd grown up in the city and done well, but there was a real working-class mentality. People were outgoing and partied a lot, but when my mother first got there, she was intimidated about becoming part of this world.

Pulling inside the stone entrance of Knollwood Country Club (established in 1894), my family was about to take a giant step up the social ladder. The valet parking attendant, dressed in a black vest and bow tie, smiled and got into our car. As he drove off, I could see the look in my mother's eyes: *How do we know he's really a valet parking attendant?*

As my father walked into the Grill Room to mingle with the men, my mother wrestled with my little sister's stroller. My brother and I seized the opportunity to begin jumping up and down on patio furniture like agitated rhesus monkeys. An old battle-ax named Joan O'Connel took one look at the grandchildren of the potato famine and said, in a loud voice, "This is what happens when they let the riffraff in."

My mother heard this and froze in humiliation. Word got back to my father in the Grill Room, and he immediately came out onto the porch. He not only dressed Mrs. O'Connel down in front of several members that day, he also coined a new nickname for this beast: "Sarge." It fit. I can't remember ever hearing anyone call her anything else. The Fitzsimmonses were here, and the country club was about to get a little riff-raffy.

The mentality of the Knollwood members is best summed up by the almost incomprehensible relationship that Willie Galloway, the archetypal black man working in the shoe-shine room, had with the members' children. It is here that the archetype shifts dramatically. Willie was encouraged to discipline members' children as he saw fit. This included, and I am not exaggerating, ample use of a bullwhip if he found that you had made a mess in his locker room. For more serious offenses (are you still with me?), Willie would come up behind you and Taser you with a cattle prod like in COPS except in this case the criminals are upper-middle-class children and the police officer is deranged from inhaling shoe polish all day. The parents thought this was absolutely hilarious.

I was forced onto the swim team, which worked out poorly, as I had a strange inability to float. This was caused by my total lack of body fat, the result of bad Irish cooking and hyperactivity. After coming in last place in a swim meet, I was awarded the perfunctory "You're All Winners" plaque at the awards dinner. After marching up to the stage, I lunged at

A twelve-year-old Shecky Green takes the mike.

the microphone and gave a lengthy acceptance speech, thanking everyone from my parents and swim coach to the president of the United States. Fuck swimming, give me that goddamned microphone!

There was a ton of laughter in my childhood. We had family rituals that were less a result of planning than repetition. Like going to the golf range to hit a bucket of balls together with no other intention than shelling the poor bastard driving the caged-in ball cart. Sunday nights after egg salad sandwiches because my mother was too exhausted from corralling us kids during the day and partying with my dad at night, we'd settle in to watch *Kojak*. My sister and I would only see the first half of the episode until being thrown out for giggling nonstop at the fact that Telly Savalas was completely bald. This did not get less funny three seasons into the show.

Our house was built for fun. The basement was unfinished, with tile floors and enough room for us to roller-skate, play ping-pong, and construct any number of life-threatening fire hazards to play with. Many nights, when my father was in a good mood, we played games in our living room. Each game had its own Fitzsimmons twist. The card game Crazy Eights turned into a taunt festival, and goofy rules were made up on the spot and then adhered to. We would play Monopoly until after midnight, sometimes on a school night, laughing until our stomachs hurt.

April Fools' Day was a Fitzsimmons national holiday. The washer nozzle for the sink needed only a rubber band around the handle to turn it into an instant chest-scalding machine that each member of the family would fall for at least twice. Saran Wrap was hung in doorways and whoopee cushions placed under every chair. Beds were short-sheeted, alarm clocks set to three in the morning.

Babysitters stood traumatized as my brother and I played full-contact Nerf basketball and launched ourselves down the stairs on pillows with salad bowls on our heads. Many, many miles of stitches were required over the years as we fell out of trees and went through windows. At one point, the garage was lit on fire. I strongly recommend to anybody reading this book that you do not have Irish children. Go out and have sex with someone who's Dutch, Latino, or even French.

Going out to dinner with my father and mother was usually great. We'd order anything we wanted off the menu and go out with other families, usually coming home so late that our parents would carry us into the house asleep.

But some nights my father's temper or depression got in the way of the good time. My dad's dark side was fearsome and unpredictable. At six foot one, he was daunting to me and anybody else who ended up on the wrong side of him.

I cringed when someone did not treat our dad the way we knew he expected to be treated, because it revealed the limits of his liberal niceness. An exchange with a flippant waiter could quickly escalate into a stomach-turning, tense nightmare that trapped the whole family. Gas station attendants or anybody else in the service industry might suffer a debilitating dress-down from my father. The mood would never recover from an incident like this. It was not always the waiter's fault. Sometimes my father would show up to the restaurant with a black cloud over his head. I can remember car rides all the way home spent in complete silence after my father had attacked somebody whom he perceived had slighted him.

He and my mother sometimes got into heated arguments in the kitchen after we had gone went to bed. I would lie down on my room's rust-colored shag carpet with my ear next to the heating vent, trying to pluck a few words from the low murmur of conversation going on down in the living room. They talked a lot about my dad's drinking.

My sister was a perpetual ally when things got bad. Deirdre has been one of my best friends pretty much from the time she was born. If my father was my role model in the entertainment business, and my mother was the connection to the Irish sense of humor, my sister was the audience. I've never made anybody laugh as hard and as often as Deirdre. She is the person I can be the most ridiculous with.

Deirdre kept me out of a lot of trouble by grabbing letters from school out of the mailbox, covering for me, and basically acting as a buffer between my parents and me. In the classic paradigm of an alcoholic family, my sister filled out the role of youngest child to a T. She was not there to cause trouble or even demand concern. She laughed easily and at the right times so that the rest of us could be the funny ones. Naturally, I felt very protective of her.

It took a lot of curls to develop these pipes.

The first time I can remember my temper overriding my rational senses was when I found my sister in a playground being pushed around by an older kid. I had just walked off a baseball field (undoubtedly having cost my team a win) and dropped my glove, bursting into a full sprint. All I remember after that was sitting on the kid's chest swinging again and again as blood spilled down both sides of his face. My sister shrieked and pulled me off of him. I walked her home and felt a sense of calm that would forever trail my postfight rages. I defended my sister many times over the years and, come to think of it, owe a beating to a kid named Jimmy Callahan, who, despite being a friend of mine, dated Deirdre and then cheated on her. She was humiliated and hurt. I'll see you around soon, asshole.

The dormant rage encoded in my Gaelic DNA had now been brought to the surface by the intermittent assaults from my father. I was a small kid, but I had been in constant training with my brother. The few altercations I'd backed down from outside the house left a burning feeling in my gut and a resolve to always engage unless doing so would lead to absolute annihilation. In the aftermath of those concessions was a promise to myself that

I'd answer in another way, at another time, and only then could I live with my humiliation. In looking over my life (which unfortunately must be done when writing an embarrassing memoirish tome like the one you are reading), my hyperambition to succeed might well have been tied to this need for revenge. Never wanting to feel vulnerable, I felt (falsely) that I would "show them" by achieving more than they did. Today I can't even remember who "they" are.

This drive also sprung from my father's oppressive need to direct every aspect of his children's lives. There was little room for our own input when it came to jobs, colleges, and, later, careers. The most frustrating part of this dynamic was that he thought he was never wrong; it was truly "Father knows best." In this case he was less of a charming father in a 1950s sitcom, and more a suffocating bully who left each of us with zero confidence to make choices later on in our own lives.

When Irish Eyes Are Bloodshot

Although I was young, I could tell my dad was in pain. His eyes were often far away, and it was like I had two fathers: the happy, outgoing, playful dad and the isolating, grumpy dad that was often around the house.

It was just as well the lights stayed off in the "corridor of low self-esteem" since the carpeting had developed a brown line down its center running from the foyer all the way down to the bathroom. This was my father's morning route after making instant coffee and heading for his shower. His shaky hand could not control the overfilled mug, and it dripped his entire trek down the hallway.

I have snapshots in my mind of him standing in the kitchen waiting for the water to boil. With a cigarette dangling off of his lower lip, he wore a tattered yellow terry cloth bathrobe with a brown fringe along its edge. Even though he was a big man, his legs were thin and bright white from not having been in the sun for decades. His toenails were so long and brittle that he could have won a cockfight. He'd stare out the kitchen window like he desperately sought answers that would not come. I remember sneaking up to the window to check and see if there was a UFO or a pile of cash on the lawn. But there was nothing (except for his car, occasionally).

Once inside the bathroom, my father would light another cigarette and place it on the side of the tub before getting in the shower. He would lean out midshower for a couple of drags. By the time I saw the bathroom, it was empty with the sour smell of alcohol. The toilet was filled with yellow water and a Viceroy that had been sucked down to the filter.

I wondered about my dad's life and why he was so far away sometimes. His brother was the only connection I had to my dad's family. Jimmy lived in the Bowery House for much of the time I knew him. It was a straight-out-of-the-movies flophouse welfare hotel for alcoholics. It was skid row. And Jimmy was a resident by the good graces of my father, who, for most of Jimmy's life, footed the bill.

We met and said good-bye to Jimmy at restaurants. He was proud of my dad and truly enjoyed both the time with his little brother's family and the quality of the places where we ate. He called them "rug joints" because the places in which he usually ate had tile floors.

Jimmy read a lot and always brought us great books to read. I can remember devouring biographies of Martin Luther King, Jr., Nelson Rockefeller, and Pope Gregory. He brought me books about the Bible and American history. My dad was tense when Jimmy was around, and he allowed him to stay over at our house only a few times when we were younger. I remember coming downstairs one morning to find Jimmy rolled up in a throw rug like a burrito. The heat had been set too low for him, and he only had a thin blanket. I remember thinking, *Wow, this guy really loves rugs.* There were a few other incidents and Jimmy was no longer welcome in our home.

Whatever happened in my dad's young life, there was now a paradox in which he strangely resented the good life he'd provided for his own family. He commented on this often. His success in life should have been a celebration, but in some weird way he was embarrassed by it, never mentioning his financial success on the air. I often wondered if he might have been happier with a failed career but with children who'd grown strong in character for having suffered the trials and tribulations of poverty. I guess if I had to choose, I'd have taken the money coupled with the illogical resentment and misdirected anger.

A lecture from my father was, for me, an exercise in survival. When he was angry, he demanded total submission of mind and spirit. If I showed any signs of defiance, he would crush me. Inflicting fear was the only way my father knew how to exert control. As a small kid, I felt like I was completely powerless and insignificant. Especially when he called me "Gregory."

"Gregory, you think you've got it all figured out—*Look at me!*—but you're a punk kid, and you better wake up before you find out how bad things can get around here for you. You understand me? What's that smirk on your face?! I'll take it off. Don't push me."

Unfortunately, I also inherited my mother's stature, which made me a good deal smaller and weaker than my dad. My father debated with people on the radio and leaned heavily on intimidation and a highly evolved sense of logic. All of these factors, combined with the fact that he was twenty-five years older than I was, gave him a distinct advantage over me as I scrapped for shreds of self-esteem.

Over time, the way I kept my dignity was to learn the art of "fake submission." I maintained eye contact and established whatever low-status behaviors I'd learned watching wild animals on nature shows. However, my mind and imagination were on fire. I mocked him and insulted him in my head, but my face betrayed none of this. Although I did not hear a single word of what he was saying to me, I would nod when it seemed like time to nod and live to fight another day. As he rambled on about me being a thankless, disrespectful wiseass, I was countering with what would years later be very similar to the style I use on hecklers in comedy clubs: "Shut up, you big-headed drunk. I'm not afraid of you. You're bald. Look at yourself! Your belly hangs over your belt, and your legs are skinny. One more Oreo, and you will fall over!" And so on. Although this helped calm me while captured in a humiliating no-win situation, damage was being done. Anger started to build up in me at a young age.

Growing up, my father's drinking was never an issue; it just was part of a cycle that seemed normal when you didn't know any better. It started out as a great thing. My father could light up a party or a restaurant and had a way of making everybody feel funny and interesting. His ball-busting was right on the money, and people felt honored to be made fun of by Bob Fitzsimmons.

This would be followed by a period where he'd come home close to dawn, and the house smelled bad the next morning. Sheets and blankets were put in the laundry as we watched cartoons. Toward the end of that cycle, we'd be relegated to watching cartoons on the floor because my dad had been banished to the couch. This often required the cushions to spend quality time in the backyard, airing out.

The serious talks downstairs kicked in around then, and they marked the close of this cycle. My mother grew louder as Dad talked less often but more explosively. I shuddered as I listened by the heating vent, knowing that my mother was shuddering downstairs. The dialogue was lost on me; through the vent, it sounded like the adults in a *Peanuts* cartoon, but in my gut I could follow the dramatic arc of the conversation. In these late-cycle battles, she didn't back down. My mom is a tough lady, and many times in their relationship she dug in. Her threats would prevail, and Dad would start drinking soda water for a month or so. He loved her enough to know that he didn't want to lose her. He'd be grumpy for a while, and then cheerful and energetic. Then he'd ease back into wine spritzers. Bartenders in the New York area would be impressed that one human being could down thirty-seven wine spritzers in a night. Beer followed, and eventually the martinis were back in full force.

One morning, as we came downstairs to watch cartoons, there was no bad smell. There was also no Dad. Mom told us he'd had a car accident the night before and was in the hospital, but he was fine. They had left the country club in separate cars, with my mother following. Gliding under the gleaming overpass of the Union Carbide plant on the edge of town, Dad passed out behind the wheel of a 1971 Ford Country Squire station wagon. You know the one: wood paneling on the sides, with a rear section for the kids constructed like an MMA ring. No seat belts or cushioning; just steel-plated walls and steel flooring so that children could enjoy each turn of the car by sliding across its width.

Luckily, those cars were built like tanks, because my dad drove straight into a tree at about forty miles per hour. My mom drove over a hill to see her husband's car buried halfway into a tree; my dad unconscious and bleeding heavily. She flagged down another car that went on to call for help. By the time an ambulance arrived, my father was presumed dead. He had severed his jugular vein and several major arteries in his wrist, and it took paramedics several minutes to revive him and get any vital signs. He spent about a week in the hospital, and when he got out, he was scarred and shaken. And thirsty.

Letters of Prophecy to the Parents of a Comedy Bozo

Rebellion against tyrants is obedience to God.

—Ben Franklin

Sorry about that last chapter. I figured I'd lump all the 'I'm Irish and my dad drank a lot' stuff into one section to get it out of the way. The truth is, juxtaposed with the darkness was equal parts light. Although we went to church every Sunday, comedy was the true religion in my house growing up. We watched the Marx brothers, Mel Brooks, and anything else that was driven by shitting all over anyone who was in charge. Bob Hope TV specials were the first sermons I remember hearing. Then Johnny Carson became the pastor. But later in life, the Pope came along: David Letterman. Finally, someone who was truly irreverent and silly. Like the Marx brothers and Mel Brooks. We never missed Mass. My dad would love retelling jokes he'd heard at the Friars Club, and pranks were as much a part of our family's everyday life as eating. We had so many running gags that often you needed only one or two words to remind us of the bit and crack up the whole family. Somebody telling a dull story would notice other family members resting their chins on their palms and sliding their elbows off the edge of the dinner table.

While other kids picked up electric guitars and sports equipment, I was feverishly collecting comedy albums and reading anything that had the word *comedy* in it. One teacher, frustrated by my fooling around in class, would allow me to tell a joke at the end of the day if I behaved. I memorized entire comedy routines by George Carlin, Bill Cosby, and Steve Martin. I was drawn to this form of entertainment because I felt like there was a science to comedy. I struggled to understand how different sequences of words could be laid out in a way that would cause a physical reaction of laughter from people.

When I was about eleven years old, my father brought me on his radio show and asked me to recite a Steve Martin routine. I started doing a bit about being a male cheerleader, "but the other cheerleaders were so jealous, they would not use any of my cheers. Like, try to score a touchdown, you douche bags." My father immediately cut off my microphone as the phones lit up. This was AM radio in the 1970s. My father told me that I could not say "douche bag" on the air. I asked my father what a douche bag was. He told me, "You don't need to know that; just don't say it." I liked that feeling, and I wanted to know more about it.

The commitment my mother had to her kids stays with me as another very bright element from this time. One of my most loving memories of my mother involved the Roma Athletic Club in White Plains. Every Friday night for about six years, Mom took me to gymnastics classes where I frightened my instructors by performing double flips with twists with absolutely no form whatsoever. My mother knew I had a lot of energy and saw what a great outlet tumbling and jumping and challenging myself could be. So she drove me there, waited an hour and a half, and then brought me home. It made me feel special and like I had something I was good at that she supported.

Wednesday evenings Mom sent us to religious education classes held in the homes of sanctimonious parishioners who were convinced they could bring the teachings of Jesus into the hearts of the young. By the age of eleven, my friends and I were terrorizing these folks in what could be seen only as a failure on the part of the instructor. One week, Tommy Bucci and I cranked up the thermostat in Mrs. Agro's tropical fish tank, boiling her fish. The following week, Mrs. Agro seemed on the brink of a nervous breakdown when her husband came downstairs and physically threatened three of us. Just like Jesus would have. Transfiguration Church felt it was best to excommunicate several of us, so we had to take religion classes in the next town over (in a home with no fish tank or husbands with rage issues). This mirrored Moses being driven from Egypt when he got into trouble. Our church really brought the Bible to life for us.

I still managed to make my confirmation that year and chose Sebastian as my confirmation name. I asked my godmother, Ann Ward, to be my sponsor.

Ann had been around when my parents first met in Hampton Bays years before. She was in Ireland when they got married, and she was there as my godmother when I was baptized. Now I had asked her to be my sponsor for confirmation. To this day, she is the person I respect most regarding spirituality. Ann was teaching in Harlem when the heroin epidemic first hit. She responded by getting involved with Phoenix House, then one location, helping them to expand to sixteen locations in a very short time. Today Phoenix House is one of the largest substance-abuse treatment services in the United States. Following that, she moved upstate to drive a school bus for handicapped kids. For many years now, she has worked with troubled kids, both in and out of jail, trying to get them off drugs.

Now confirmed, I was, in the eyes of the Church, considered a man. In the eyes of my school, though, I appeared to be a large pain in the ass. I

My godmother, Ann, and her confirmation gift to me: a human chess piece.

59

think we all have an age that we get stuck in; an age we revisit a dispropor-
tionate number of times and when we do, strong emotions come to the
surface. For me, that time is seventh and eighth grades. Up to this point,
I'd mostly hung around with what might be considered nerdy kids. I spent
a lot of time reading and liked goofing around more than I liked organized
sports. I was becoming bored with these more passive kids though and
found myself pushing them to do crazy things like ride bicycles through
their homes, explore the roof of their house, or play "find your dad's porn
stash."

I loved the rush of excitement, whether it was building a bike ramp as
tall as I was and hitting it full speed only to land sideways on the pavement
or climbing up the sides of buildings. I was a regular at the emergency
room and am stitched together like a shorter, more angry version of Frank-
enstein.

In seventh grade, I began hanging around a group of more popular, confident, and wild kids. I felt unworthy, and I spent a lot of time trying to earn
my spot with crazy stunts that made everybody laugh. I often put my life in
danger as an offering to my friends. The picture over there is me hanging by
my knees from my friend Brian's fifth-floor balcony.

Along the way, I sometimes threw some of my former nerd friends
under the bus. Mark Rossignol was one of my original friends that I felt I
was "outgrowing," and he was soon in the crosshairs of my new friends'
cruelty. We would prank call his house after school. After he admitted that
he was a fan of the band the Knack, we began singing "My Sharona" every
time he walked by and challenged him to fight daily. The harassment got to
the point that his mom came to school and spoke with the principal. On the
way out of his office, she saw me in the hallway, put her finger in my face,
and said, "You're on the top of the list." I laughed in front of my friends as
she stormed out, but there was a rock in the pit of my stomach as I thought
about how this woman used to make homemade pizza for me after school. I
started pushing it further with teachers, and soon my parents were opening
a lot of notes sent home from school.

Once my parents stopped laughing, there would sometimes be a lecture.
My father would say, "Gregory, you've got a real attitude. You think you

Flipping off a wall with my buddy Kyle, now the judge in Tarrytown.

Dear Mrs. Fitzsimmons

Patricia Fitzsimmons
123 Fourth Street
Westchester, NY 10500

DISCIPLINARY NOTICE

Student: Greg Fitzsimmons

Section: 8 E

Date: 10/12/80

Description of Incident:

Greg was loitering in the hallway on Wednesday with several
other students when I walked by on my way home. Greg then began
openly mocking me by making fun of my name (i.e. "The grass looked very
Dewey this morning", "Dewey have any homework?" and "Are we going to
learn the Dewey Decimal System?").

At first I ignored him, but eventually I felt I needed to take
some action. It is disrespectful and rude to address a teacher in such
a manner and I think it best to bring this to his parent's
attention.

Faculty Member: Dewey Ekdahl

Signature: Dewey Ekdahl   Date:

Parent Signature: Patricia Fitzsimmons   Date:

know better than everyone else. Someday that will serve you well. Hang on to that. But for now, shut up and do what you are told."

Changing my attitude felt like something I wanted to have control of. But I could not. Once I became angry or felt slighted, there was little I could do to control my actions. There was (and still is) a switch that I have little access to, despite myself.

So for those of you keeping score at home: my authority figure encouraged me to think for myself, to behave, yet to keep a rebellious spirit underneath a false sense of conformity. Add to that a "get out of jail free" card if you get a laugh. Not too many more dots to connect before I am traveling from town to town seeking approval from drunken strangers in comedy clubs.

Another element that would have a profound influence on me also emerged at this time. At around twelve years old, two friends and I found an unopened bottle of Genesee Cream Ale lying under the bleachers during a football game. We slipped into the woods, popped it open, and each sucked down a third of the beer. I can still remember the warm, tingly sensation that instantly went through my body. I liked it a lot. My commitment to this new liquid was immediate. Over the next fourteen years, we would spend a lot of time together.

The awkwardness of puberty, acne, insecurity, and self-hatred now had a short-term solution. Whatever social anxiety challenged me could be conquered by a cold beer or a warm joint. Pot felt good, but alcohol was the perfect antidote—it was what my people did well. Along with drinking were the alcoholic activities common to suburban teenagers: long stretches of acute boredom broken up by acts of vandalism.

My friends and I were like ants, constantly scrambling and scouring for alcohol, drugs, or anything that could bring some excitement. Vandalism gave me a focus for my anger. By seventh grade, a typical day involved looking for things to break. Vandalism was somehow intertwined in every activity. Stickball at the high school? Smash a window at the end of the game. Wednesday evening religion class? Smoke a joint and pull a fire alarm on the way there. Visiting a friend's house? Take a shit in his neighbor's mailbox. Destroy a mailbox with a baseball bat.

VILLAGE JUSTICE'S COURT — ☐
POLICE DEPARTMENT — ☒
Village of Tarrytown
150 Franklin Street
Tarrytown, N.Y.

Nº 13774

Date _July 7_, 19_80_

Received from _Juvenile-case Fitz Simmons_
the sum of _Thirty Four 00/_ $ _34.00_, for Bail ☐ — Fine ☐
for violation of Sec. _____ Subd. _____

Restitution in Reference to Complaint D #80-478
Victim - J. Schessel, Cobb Lane

Police Reg. No.
Meter Ordinance . . . . ☐
Village Ordinance . . . . ☐
V. & T. Law . . . . ☐
Penal Law . . . . ☐
C. C. P. . . . . ☐

A.O. Richard Pollini - Youth officer
(Village Justice) (Clerk)

This fine came after my arrest for destroying a neighbor's pool by heaving a large flower pot in it. I have absolutely no idea why.

I can't help but think, as I look back, that the bad letters sent home had created some real issues with mailboxes. (If so, I need to get in touch with my rage against toilets, as well.)*

By the age of twelve, my friends and I became very friendly with the Tarrytown police. Page three of the local paper was where the police blotter usually appeared. On certain mornings, I would race to get the newspaper first. By the time my parents read it, there might be a square cut out of page three. I saved these cut-outs like trophies.

Roughly every other month, page three had a blurb on our neighbor Terrance Mahoney's bike. Terrance often carelessly left his bike in his garage. I would sneak through the garage window and then ride the bike into town when I went out at night. The cops would find it and return it to the Mahoneys. It wasn't a perfect system, but I felt that it worked pretty well.

In seventh grade, Washington Irving Junior High School accidentally assigned six of the most ill-behaved kids in school to the same class. Most of the teachers were prepared for us, having dealt with our older brothers or sisters over the years. They'd developed techniques to conquer and

---

* The use of parenthesis in this book often relays my lack of confidence in a joke—or your ability to get it.

Police file

Caleb Raul Quinoy, 41, 44 Depeyster St., North Tarrytown, was charged at his home Saturday at 5:55 p.m. with harassment, police said, following a family dispute. He was released on his own recognizance pending a Thursday court date.

Theft

Donald Mahoney, 34, of Suncliff Drive, Tarrytown reported Sunda at 2:44 pm. a bicycle was stolen from his garage.

The Mahoney family didn't like us. We often stole their bicycles.

humiliate rabid boys who were simultaneously hitting puberty and each other.

Mrs. Leonard, however, was the weak link. She was a blond-haired, blue-eyed young woman who drove a Mercedes to school and probably imagined that exposing adolescents to literature would be an inspiring experience. Instead she found herself breaking up fights and dealing with a classroom full of morons.

One day's lesson was about phonetics. Mrs. Leonard took a stick and pointed to different vowel and consonant sounds on a large wall chart. She then asked us to spell words using the correct phonetic symbols. Raising my hand, there was already snickering in the back row. She warily handed me the stick, and I pointed to the letter *p*, followed by the letter *u*. Do I even have to continue? I then pointed to *s* and another *s*. By now, kids could barely control themselves. Norman and Brian were doubled over in their seats, knowing as well as Mrs. Leonard that the pointer was on its way to the letter *y*. Finishing the word *pussy* created an explosion of laughter like two cymbals crashing together. I handed the pointer back to Mrs. Leonard and calmly walked back to my seat, my face giving nothing away. Mrs. Leonard turned red, pursed her lips, and walked down the aisle to my desk. She said, "I know exactly what you meant." This only doubled the laughter and cemented the stoic look on my face. I was embarrassed that I had done this to

Mrs. Leonard, but my friends were laughing, and that was more important.

A lot of the pranks were less mean and more ridiculous. For five consecutive days, my friends and I would buy a six pack of Mountain Dew and a dozen donuts. We would then stand in front of the plate glass window in front of Adam and Eve hair salon and shove everything down our faces to the horror of the women inside. One morning, the principal announced over the loudspeaker that Adam and Eve would no longer be honoring our school's discount card. Laughter spilled out of homeroom classes all over the school.

On warm days, the windows of Dr. Quinn's ground-floor classroom would be flung open to the bustling traffic on Broadway. At least once a week, one of us would slip out the window while Dr. Quinn was drawing on the board. Upon our return fifteen or twenty minutes later, Dr. Quinn would ask where we had been. The rest of the class would remind Dr. Quinn that he'd excused us to go to the bathroom. He would look confused but then move on with the lesson.

Often when he would turn his back to write on the blackboard, half the class would immediately stand up on their chairs and then sit back down again. He would spin around, wondering why everybody was laughing, to see thirty students were sitting with their hands folded on their desks. Other mornings he would walk in to find Head & Shoulders shampoo on his desk in response to the avalanche of white flakes that landed on his red plaid blazer every afternoon. Dr. Quinn would jog in Patriots Park early in the morning. One morning before school, we hid underneath the bridge near the track and pelted Dr. Quinn with slingshots.

By eighth grade, I found myself on a lot of lists in school. Before this time, I'd been on lists for advanced reading and school drama. Now I was on lists for school detention and behavioral problems. In the spring, Mrs. Leonard asked five of us to meet with her after school. She told us she knew we were getting high a lot and that pot would lead to more serious drugs like cocaine. She was actually pretty cool about sitting down with us instead of calling in our parents or alerting the principal. We all laughed about it afterward. Within a couple of years, we were all tripping on mescaline, mushrooms, and experimenting with cocaine. I blame Mrs. Leonard for not having sent us to the principal.

Soon thereafter, the seventh-grade class went on a field trip to Washington,

DC. After several fire alarms had been pulled and many reports from hotel security about teenagers drinking and vandalizing in the hotel, Mr. Thomas, our social studies teacher, set up individual interrogation sessions back at the school. The math teacher, Mr. Scrocka, simultaneously set up individual interrogations with the same students. They invoked the classic routine of telling us, "Your friends all admitted you were drinking, so you might as well also, because if you don't, you'll be the only one to get in trouble."

My friends folded like a house of cards, but I had seen that episode of *Dragnet* and held my ground, insisting, "I have no idea what anybody else did, but I know that *I* did not drink on that trip." Truthfully, I drank a lot on that trip: gin straight out of shampoo bottles (that could have been rinsed a lot better before we put in the gin. I remember vomiting not far from the Lincoln Memorial, and the chunks of cheeseburger from dinner were barely visible beneath the froth of shampoo bubbles).

My particular class proved to be too much for the teachers to handle. The field trip was the last straw, and four of us were pulled out of class and dispersed among the other seventh-grade classes.

Tarrytown was a cool place with a lot of history and now a lot of diversity. It was around this time that our school was asked to participate in a project where we created a motto for Tarrytown. Kyle (now the judge) coined the winning slogan: "We are the world's melting pot." The community was a melting pot in every sense of the word. While my family had a nice house at the top of the hill and belonged to a country club, my best friend was Mike Gonzalez, whose Colombian dad, Horatio, raised him upstairs from a bodega on Cortland Street. By the age of eleven, Mike had hit puberty and unofficially became the bodyguard of a skinny Irish kid (that would be me). He was also looking after his own father at this point. Horatio was a maître d' at a steak restaurant in nearby Ossining. He drank a lot, and Mike would often have to pile him in the back of their van and drive him home.

Mike's older brother, Hector, showed me my first porn movie. Unfortunately, this was prior to my mother's telling me about the birds and the bees. I'm not sure what was more confusing: the violent movements of the couples grinding against each other, the erection I had, or the fact that Hector kept grabbing the erection.

Seventh and eighth grades caused a big ripple in the melting pot. As we got older, groups started to form more on the basis of skin color than friendship. I used to hang around with a guy named Dwayne Davis. He was a black kid whose nickname was Snoopy long before Snoop Dog. (Not trying to start another "East Coast–West Coast" thing, I'm just saying . . .)

Dwayne and I had a "bit" we liked to do. He was much larger than me, so I would walk up to him and order him around. He would act afraid of me and do whatever I said. One day, I approached Snoopy, now in seventh grade, as he stood among some black kids from eighth grade. I learned a very important lesson in comedy that day: context is everything. I started the bit and immediately became puzzled as Snoop seemed to forget his lines. I raised the stakes on my end to help him out, dropping a pen and demanding that he pick it up. At this point, Snoop picked me up, held me upside down, and dropped me on my back. I lay on the ground with the wind knocked out of me, looking at Dwayne, confused and scared. They all laughed as they walked off, although I remember Snoop looking back for a split second to see if I was all right. Apparently no one had remembered to send me the rewrite that had been done on the bit, but I felt the old version was funnier. And less painful. Then again, I had never sent Marc Rossignal the changes I'd made to our script . . .

The Eisners from down the block were neighbors and had two kids around my age. By the eighth grade, they were both forbidden to hang out with my brother and me. I believe my brother had gone to at least second base with their daughter Susan, and Coach Dr. Eisner had pulled her out of the game before Team Fitzsimmons could make it all the way home. Although I still liked the Eisner kids, being on another list felt less like an embarrassment than a badge of honor. One day, a kid named Jeff Singer was harassing Susan Eisner. This should not have been a big concern to me, since there was an embargo on our friendship, but whenever I saw a girl or a weaker kid being harassed, something in me always snapped. It still does. I punched Jeff Singer in the face, knocking his glasses to the ground, and then I threw him around in front of a large group of kids getting off the bus.

It was more than his actions deserved, but he was a nerd and not much bigger than I was. Jeff was always a little odd, and several years later, we found out that it was more than that. He drove his car down a deserted road behind the Tarrytown Lakes, scribbled satanic messages onto the windows, and then ran a hose from his exhaust pipe into the car. His parents taught religious education in Tarrytown, and it was hard to imagine what this must have been like for them. I still carry around the shame from knowing that I contributed in any way to making this kid's life harder than it already must have been.

My summer days were spent mostly at Knollwood Country Club. The place was soon less about enjoyments and entitlement for me as it was about trying to make some money. Because of the large membership of Italians at the club, my father nicknamed Knollwood "Cannoli Wood." From ages ten to twelve, I assisted Willie Galloway (the nice gentleman with the cattle prod) in shining the members' shoes. When it started to rain, the parking attendants pulled me from the shoe room and paid me to run around rolling up car windows. The worst job at that time, though, was shagging golf balls. I would imagine that shagging balls is now considered a felony in America. A frightened eleven-year-old is put in the middle of a driving range while a grown man hits balls at him. The boy then ducks and covers his head before running over and putting the balls in a sack. It was bad, but it was a gateway to becoming a caddy.

At thirteen years old, I weighed approximately twenty-six pounds. Having graduated to the caddy yard, I would be handed, on a hot summer day, a 125-pound leather bag containing not just clubs but enough extra balls to open a sporting goods store. For five straight hours, I would do so much damage to my back and skin that, to this day, I am dealing with doctors' offices all over Los Angeles. As the worst golfers in New York state shanked balls deep into the trees, my job was to dart around the deer tick–infested woods and come out with the ball. That, or face the anger of the seventy-six-year-old dentist with an alcohol problem.

Because I was a member's son, Bobby Ormonde, the caddy master, delighted in assigning me bad golfers with large bags and anemic wallets. I believe my father was in on the joke. Mr. Barone was, in the caddy world, the equivalent of childhood AIDS. He was my regular loop. My father liked to see that I was working, but I think he enjoyed even more that I was not enjoying a country club life that I so richly did not deserve. Caddying was also a very convenient way for my father to punish me on the mornings he knew I'd been out drinking late.

Early one August morning, my father roused me from a two-hour Jack Daniel's coma. Twenty minutes later I was sitting on a railroad tie in the caddy yard waiting for what I hoped would be a fatal stroke. My head was spinning, and I would've thrown up, but I'm pretty sure I got most of it out about four hours earlier while stumbling home. My worst nightmare appeared before me: Mr. Barone, walking shoulder to shoulder with Mr. Connors, Mr. Lowen, and Mr. Mueller—the Four Horsemen of Cheap. The grumpiest and least co-ordinated bastards ever assembled were to be my loop for the day.

After seven holes of lugging and straining and searching and holding my tongue, my thighs were done. I waved to Mr. Barone to indicate that yet another one of his drives went out of bounds. There are out-of-bounds balls that can be retrieved and there are out-of-bounds balls that are in a backyard getting chewed by a rabid German shepherd. When Mr. Barone made his way down the fairway, he asked, "Where the hell is my goddamn ball?" I dropped the bag, looked him in the eye, and said, "How the hell should I know? You hit the fucking thing." I didn't even wait to be fired; I turned on my heel and exited the golf course knowing I could not go on. When I got to the clubhouse, I expected Bob Ormonde and my father to be waiting along with Willie Galloway and the cattle prod. Instead I was regaled by caddies and a dozen members of the club—including my father—who gave me a round of applause. I had graduated. It was the last time I caddied for Mr. Barone.

At night, I would be out with my friends in town, or they would come over to my house while my parents were out. We spent a lot of time hang-ing around places with names like "the Hot Spot," "Frog Rock," "the Spot," "the Bleachers," and "Bong Bridge." At the time, I never thought much about what drew us together, but looking back, there were things we all had in common: we'd rather be out than at home, and we partied more than anyone else—except for our parents.

My parents were beginning to get concerned about my behavior, but more so about the public high school. It was not good. It was pretty bad,

Washington Irving Junior High School
TARRYTOWN, NEW YORK

NAME: Gregory Fitzsimmons

PROGRESS REPORT: 1979-80

CONGRATULATIONS! Honor Roll.

A MESSAGE TO PARENTS:

Together we have an equal interest and responsibility for your child's education. We invite you to call the Counseling Office at 631-9400, extension 243 whenever you have a question about your son's or daughter's school progress. Appointments can be easily arranged with your child's counselor or teachers at a convenient time. An unsatisfactory report should be, of course, a cause of individual concern, but we welcome your questions about any matter of curriculum or school operation at any time.

HOMEROOM 109 GRADE 8p-1 COUNSELOR Dr. Gibian

SUBJECT	PROGRESS 1	2	3	4	EXAM	FINAL GRADES	LEVELS 1	2	3	4	BEHAVIOR 1	2	3	4	EFFORT 1	2	3	4	PERIODS ABSENT 1	2	3	4
ENGLISH	90	92						2				1					2				3	
SOCIAL STUDIES	70	88					2	2			2	2			2	2			1		3	
MATHEMATICS	85	95					2	2			3	3			2	2			0		2	
SCIENCE	88	87					2	2			2	2			2	2			0		5	
PHYSICAL EDUCATION	83	85					2	2			3	2			3	2			5		6	
ART EDUCATION	81				81		2				3				2				0			
MUSIC EDUCATION																						
INDUSTRIAL ARTS		80			80		2				2				2				5			
HOME ECONOMICS		82			82		2				2				2				1			
HEALTH EDUCATION																						
Language Skills	90	94				1	1				2	3			2	2			0		2	

EXPLANATION OF CODES

GRADING KEY	EXPLANATION OF LEVELS:	BEHAVIOR:	EFFORT:
90-100 = Excellent Progress	1. Working at a level of achievement above that expected of the average student in this grade.	1 - COMMENDABLE	1 HIGH INTEREST & EFFORT
88-89 = Above Average Progress			
75-79 = Average Progress	2. Working at the level of achievement expected of the typical or average student in this grade (i.e., 7th grade student is working at 7th grade level).	2 - SATISFACTORY	2 GOOD INTEREST & EFFORT
70-74 = Acceptable Progress			
65-69 = Low Acceptable Progress		3 - NEEDS IMPROVEMENT	3 WEAK INTEREST & EFFORT
64 and Below = Little or No Progress	3. Working at a level of achievement below that expected of the average student in this grade.		
I = Incomplete		4 - UNSATISFACTORY	4 UNSATISFACTORY

actually. Not just academically, but there was a fair amount in the newspaper about the drugs and trouble that went on there. My parents knew me well enough to know that although I got in a lot of trouble, there was something inside me that did not go over the line. I made my own money and, up to that point, had always kept my grades up.

While my grades were consistently high, so was I. My parents were convinced that keeping me in public school after eighth grade would be a huge mistake. They felt that the best thing for me was to spend time away from my Tarrytown friends and get a good education at a private high school.

Looking around Westchester, nothing seemed appealing until I got to Rye Country Day School. It had a hockey rink. What could possibly go wrong?

They were about to find out.

That's Not Where I Wanna Be

I hid in the clouded wrath of the crowd, but when they said "Sit down,"

I stood up. Ooh-ooh, growin' up.

—"Growin' Up," Bruce Springsteen

Returning to the premise that my father resented his children for being so well provided for (by him), let's go back to 1980. His disgust with the good fortune he'd provided was taken to new heights as he sent his children to private high schools.

Truthfully, I didn't really appreciate how good we did have it. Our home was not broken, we had a big house that both of my parents lived in, we belonged to a country club, and went on vacations. But as I got older, it became increasingly obvious to me that I was, as John Fogerty once sang, a "fortunate son." A lot of my friends lived with single parents in pretty run-down apartments. Some were well off like my family, but nobody really made a big deal about where anyone was from. Entering this toney prep school in ninth grade, I found myself in an awkward middle ground. I was suddenly poor. The student parking lot in Tarrytown looked like an impound station in the South Bronx. Those early-model Chevy Monte Carlos or rusted-out station wagons were often stuffed with six to ten kids chasing down pot, alcohol, or girls from out of town who didn't know yet.

Kids from Rye, however, cruised to school confidently behind the wheels of BMWs, Mercedes, and Saabs; one girl even owned a DeLorean (I believe her father owned the company). My new peers came from families that owned things. Things like one of Manhattan's hottest nightclubs. The school body watched in horror as the father was convicted on felony tax evasion.

Tarrytown kids had names like Strange Dave, Dido, Alphonse, Johnny Trouble, Twitch, Mike the Bug, Spags, and Hector. Now I was at Rye Country Day with a kid named Randolph Van Kleet III. He dated a girl named Ashley Briggs. I believe they married and had a child, on the deck of the *Mayflower*, who came out with a perfect set of teeth and a 4 handicap in golf. Roone Arledge Jr., whose father ran ABC News at that time, went to my school, whose alumni included Barbara Bush (class of 1807) and actor Christopher Atkins, whose blond locks spilled over a half-naked fifteen-year-old Brooke Shields in the movie *The Blue Lagoon*.

One of my friends was named Jeff Van Stratten; there were a lot of "Vans" at RCDS. Not the kind of vans found in a parking lot. The kind of Vans found in the middle of their surname to show their Dutch pedigree.

RYE COUNTRY DAY SCHOOL

Gregory Fitzsimmons	French I	2/23/81
STUDENT	COURSE	DATE

12 11 10 (9)		F
GRADE		MARK

Although Greg had been inching upward during the second semester, he has virtually ceased working altogether in French this quarter.

His quizzes show virtually no preparation either in learning vocabulary items or verb forms, two areas that require nothing more than rote memorization. Greg must do a minimum of work in this course!

Mr. Brown	
ADVISOR	SIGNATURE

Instead of feeling like everybody else, I felt low-class. I didn't know what lacrosse was, we did not have live-in help, and I didn't appear to have sprung from the cover of a J. Crew catalog. Apart from the social rejection I was feeling at Rye Country Day, there was the academic failure confirmed almost immediately by my horrible test scores.

Each day started badly. In the morning I'd walk to the public high school, where I'd slump onto a large yellow school bus provided for kids attending schools in other districts. In the parking lot, I'd see my friends huddled around a joint before homeroom. Instead of joining them (because I was always late), I'd board the bus. I sat among seventy-five Catholic school girls attending parochial schools around Westchester. I was the only boy on the bus. As a forty-four-year-old man, that sounds like act one, scene one of a high-end porn film, but when you're a redheaded fourteen-year-old boy with the body of an eleven-year-old girl, it is a very awkward and painful daily commute. Some of the girls were very cute, and their adolescent sexuality was highlighted by the crisp white linen shirts and plaid miniskirts. I've never understood the philosophy behind dressing young women you are

RYE COUNTRY DAY SCHOOL		
Fitzsimmons, Gregory	French I	2/19/1982
STUDENT	COURSE	DATE
12 11 (10) 9		D plus
GRADE		MARK

Although Greg has been making an evident effort to control his disruptive attitude, he has not yet developed the maturity to understand his role as a student and, too often, acts as a seventh grader. He is never thoroughly attentive in class, and the quality of his tests and quizzes reveals a lack of concentration and a superficial knowledge of the materials. Even if Greg passes this course - which I am doubting at this point - he will not have acquired the basic foundations that would enable him to pursue the study of the language successfully.
As the saying goes, however, it is never too late ...... and I hope that Greg will soon realize his responsibilities as a student and understand what is expected of him.

Mr. Brown		J. Anselly
ADVISOR		SIGNATURE

2/18/82

Mr. & Mrs. Robert Fitzsimmoms
27 Walden Road
Tarrytown, NY 10591

Dear Mr. and Mrs. Fitzsimmons:

Last week I had a long talk with Greg about a couple
of teachers who were seriously concerned about his behavior in class. Mrs. Amsellem is still not entirely
satisfied, even though he has not got any worse. But
this time, Mrs. Solomon (geometry) said that he has begun to misbehave in her class. We talked about the
reasons for his being more cooperative--his own grade,
and the effect it has on other students in particular
--and he seemed to be serious and understanding at the
time. I said that the teachers had requested me to write
his parents to show our concern. I thought he was impressed enough with our conference for me to leave him on
his own and not get trouble here and at home as well.
Then I get the enclosed report.

I am the very last person to say that our classes
should not occasionally be humorous and even be a bit
of fun. But Greg goes too far. He is getting a bad
name for himself even from those teachers who do not
know him. I hate to see this happen. But I have to put
him on warning now that he is in danger of not being
invited back here for his eleventh grade year simply
because of absurd behavior of this kind. There is too
much at stake: the teachers do not have time to deal with
such immaturity; the other students' education is being
disrupted. I sincerely hope that he can show us his best
side in the next few weeks. I do not want to ask him not
to return; maybe I am too soft with him, but I find him
a likeable person. (Perhaps I should have him in class.)

Sincerely,

Glen Robertson
Dean of Boys

---

trying to keep chaste in costumes left over from a Van Halen video. Maybe it was an effort to get the priests to stop paying so much attention to the boys. Looking back, their plan failed miserably.

On many, many, many, many, mornings I missed my bus. Psychologists will tell you that being late is passive-aggressive. People who are late are bucking the social contract. But there is one authority that is impossible to fight: Father Time. And yet my entire life, I have done so. Missing the

RYE COUNTRY DAY SCHOOL		
Fitzsimmons, Gregory	Biology	10/27
STUDENT	**COURSE**	**DATE**
9		D−
GRADE		**MARK**

Gregory's average in Biology at the moment is 60. His homework papers have been generally good but his test and quiz averages are failing. Greg sits in the back of the class and has been known, on occasion, to drift off towards sleep. Of course all this is of great concern to me as his teacher and of double concern as his advisor when I hear the same kinds of comments coming from other teachers. Of late, however, Greg has shown some signs of life. I am convinced that he has much ability that he has yet to use. Now the question is, does he have the desire to get himself out of the predicament he is in?

Mr. Brown

Richard Brown

TEACHER SIGNATURE

bus required that I walk a mile to a public bus stop, change buses in White Plains, and then wait for a train to take me from Port Chester to Rye. This made me late for school, requiring that I come to school the next morning at seven for early-morning detention. There is no fucking way I ever made it to early-morning detention on time, which required my presence at Saturday morning detention. (Rent the movie *The Breakfast Club,* then replace the "brat pack" with the teen crew of a yacht.) Would I be late for this? Of course. I was on a roll.

I realized as I got older that my parents were as intimidated by RCDS as I was. These were the richest families with the smartest kids. In Tarrytown, I would have been considered a nice kid with good grades. Here I was a failure and an outlaw.

The cultural foundation of my low self-esteem primed me to absorb these cues of inferiority like a confused, freckled sponge. I hated some of those kids like I'd never hated anyone before. In my life prior to this, rejection came in the form of a beating or insults that I could at least engage in. I didn't mind that. Now, however, I was exposed to a phantom: class rejection. I was not invited to parties or flirted with, or taken seriously in any way. Trudging to school in a pair of Timberlands bought with a discount because of the sole projecting an inch ahead of the boot and a ski hat with the Harlem Globetrotters' logo on it did not garner me access among these athletic kids in Izods who seemed to have not a care in the world.

Just to set the record straight, my family was upper-middle-class. I was one of the lucky kids in my town, so it is hard to describe how I could be made to feel so inferior. Having undiagnosed ADHD led to me staring off into space, unable to focus on an entire lesson in any class. I failed to make the baseball team three years in a row, and by senior year I was the captain of the junior varsity hockey team. I don't think that's even legal. It's like sneaking in to the Special Olympics because you have a hangnail.

I was relegated to hanging with kids from unfashionable towns like Eastchester, White Plains, and Elmsford. We drafted several members of the school aristocracy: boys who'd lost their way and been rejected from the alpha pack. We formed and excelled in underage intoxication. Lunchtime was an opportunity to leave campus and drive either into Port Chester for fast food or to the mansion of one of the rich kids, where a black maid would make us food. We'd ride dirt bikes around their estate before going back to school high as a kite and full of expensive filet mignon sandwiches. I felt socially rejected throughout the day in school, and returning to Tarrytown usually involved stopping at a friend's house to feel normal before going home. I needed to feel like I belonged.

What connected my friends and I was an energy that sprung from a need to express ourselves and to fight back against anyone in charge. Often this was born out of a troubled home life but I doubt any of us would have described it that way at the time because it was just that way. Running into a friend's dad at a local dive bar or seeing a friend's mom with a highball at noon never seemed odd. The fact that our parents all drank, took pills, and smoked weed was just part of the culture in which we grew up. We laughed about beatings we received or seeing a friend's mother passed out in their living room.

I started high school in 1980, but the Rye kids—dressed in the timeless style often seen in retirement homes in Florida—listened to the soulless bourgeois anthems of James Taylor, UB40, and Jorma Kaukonen. Back in Tarrytown kids had long hair and listened only to music that was made between 1966 and 1973. We split our time between the principal's office, the police station, and houses of kids whose parents were absent.

We logged many productive hours at Marymount College, a Catholic school for women. It sat on top of the hill in Tarrytown, just a few blocks from my house. Identifying a spiritually challenged undergraduate could easily have been a varsity sport for us. I remember, as a thirteen-year-old, drinking Boone's Farm strawberry wine with my buddy Sean Carney and a Dominican theology student from Marymount. She took turns sipping from the bottle and making out with each of us. Our unfettered access to the campus could be attributed to the lax efforts of the Marymount security guard, who was also the older brother of one of my friends. The foxes were

Friends don't let friends wear plaid.

> "Two weeks ago the building was severely spray-painted by students, probably chemically-dependent," said one teacher, who said certain teachers had already been called "narcs" by students.

In case the statute of limitations has not expired, I have no idea how this clipping got into my book.

in the henhouse, and the hens were drunkenly dry humping local teenagers (many of whom were not even Catholic).

On the nights that I was grounded, which seemed more often than not, my open window brought in the punishing sounds of young people's laughter mixed with breaking glass and squealing tires. My loneliness on these nights had a soundtrack thanks to the records of Bruce Springsteen. From the defiance of "Growing Up" through the fleeting escape found on "Racing in the Street"—these songs validated my sense not only of rejection, but of what I had rejected. I drifted off to sleep knowing that how I felt in that moment was how I would always feel. Some choices lie ahead but others had already been made.

The alienation was made all the more resonant because Bruce had to remain my guilty pleasure. My friends mocked the concept of Springsteen, a Jersey greaseball. I felt the same way until I stumbled on the album *Darkness on the Edge of Town* inside a random brown box. My father received these shipments daily from record companies trying to promote artists and get them more radio play. Though Bruce would never be in rotation on WNEW-AM, WNEW-FM honored him with a daily segment called "Bruce Juice."

Bruce's songs told of growing up beside a river; in my case, the mighty Hudson. In the shadow of the Tappan Zee Bridge, we huddled in our cars pooling money for an eight-pack, a bag of weed, or, on a really luxurious night, a gram of cocaine. We started hanging out at "the benches." The benches were located in front of Baskin-Robbins, presumably for patrons to sit with their children and enjoy a precious eating-ice-cream-with-their-child moment.

Instead the benches hosted teenagers waiting like migrant workers outside of a Home Depot. We prayed for somebody old enough to drive and lucky enough to have a car that night. Prior to arriving at the benches, I would light a Marlboro and increase the height of my gait by about a quarter of an inch. I'd blend in with Johnny Trouble, Strange Dave, and a confederacy of Irish knuckleheads called only by their last names: McGovern, McDonald, Donahue, and Kelleher.

At sixteen, my mother taught me how to drive, and my father introduced

Me and my freedom bus, a '76 Volkswagen Rabbit.

me to road rage. He drove Lincoln Town Cars. Big, leathery Mafia-looking Town Cars. One day, while lining up to pay the toll at the Triborough Bridge, my father engaged in a battle of wills with a merging taxi. Dad rolled down his window, and with a Viceroy cigarette dangling from his lip, he quietly told the cab driver that if he touched our car, my father would rip his throat out. The taxi driver yielded. This was one of dozens of experiences in a car where I thought it entirely possible that I would be killed with my father behind the wheel. He passed the torch to me, and I proudly carry on the tradition of illogical road rage in its capital: Los Angeles, California.

In my junior year of high school, I took $800 of my caddying savings and bought a brown 1976 Volkswagen Rabbit. It became a chamber of dreams for me. I drank in it, smoked in it, listened to Talking Heads and Led Zeppelin at a blistering half decibel through the one cracked speaker, and then smoked again. It allowed me to get to and from high school without relying on the school bus or public transportation. The car was a piece of shit. The floorboards had rusted through, and after big rainstorms, there would be upward of ten gallons of water swishing around the floor (which was about double what was in the tank). One winter, the water froze, and, until the spring thaw, I drove with a block of ice under my feet.

Without exception, and I became known for this move—I would pick up friends, and then fifty feet into the trip I would stop the car and say, "I hate to be a dick, but can I get a couple of bucks for gas?"

Following an "incident" one weekend, my parents told me that I could not drive my car to school for a month. I began secretly driving to school anyway without their knowledge, claiming that the car was being repaired by a friend. I was busted when a friend called the house wondering when I would be picking him up. There was a pretty major brawl. I felt like I had earned the right to drive and the car was being taken away by people who hadn't given it to me in the first place. Fortunately, the Rabbit caught on fire soon after, and the issue blew over.

If the car represented a way for me to get away from my parents, it was far from it. Because Dad's voice was on so many radio commercials, he was seemingly omnipresent. After hours of negotiating one night, I sat with my hand up Tracey Secunda's shirt. My father suddenly burst into the front seat extolling the virtues of Uncle Ben's rice. I swore off that rice for the rest of my life. Although I still am quite fond of breasts.

My mother had little intuition when it came to my sex life. I can remember her explaining the birds and the bees to me shortly after the first time I had sex. Considering the fact that she was more nervous telling me about it than I was actually doing it, it must have been one of the most difficult things she'd ever done. I would have spared her, except I wanted to know if I was doing it right. Afterward she told me, "Now don't *ever* tell your grandfather I told you that."

The process of losing my virginity began a couple of months before the act actually transpired. At around age 15, my buddy, Sean Carney and I made a bet about who would lose his virginity first. The $20 wager had a clause built into it: the bet was off if the second imbecile lost his virginity within thirty days of the first imbecile. Six months into the bet, I was informed by my nemesis that I'd lost. The young lady, Stacey Movetti, was from the next town and had already generously bedded many of our friends. I congratulated Sean, reminding him that he was a month away from collecting.

A week later, hanging out at the benches with Johnny Trouble, Lisa Leone's blue 1974 Pontiac Trans Am pulled up with Stacey Movetti riding shotgun. Johnny and I boarded the vessel, and an hour later parked on a muddy road in Elmsford with the romantic buzzing of power lines above our heads. While Johnny Trouble and Lisa rocked the Camaro on the trunk (for less than sixty-seconds), I leaned on the hood with my pants around my ankles. With my feet slipping in the mud, I became a man with the same woman that Sean had been with seven days earlier. When I told Sean that I'd neutralized the bet, I lied about who I'd been with. We laughed and then played Frisbee for three hours.

My friends and I never really felt like badasses, because so many of the guys around us were much tougher and much crazier. Beekman Avenue was where they hung out and the worst were known as "the Gravediggers." Funny story how they got their unusual nickname. High on angel dust one night, they'd gone to the graveyard and exhumed a recently buried body out of the loose dirt. They took body parts and played football with them. Apparently this is a felony, and they all did time for it. When they returned they reassembled on the same corner, listening to the same Black Sabbath albums and creeping the shit out of everybody in Tarrytown for years to come. These guys started and ended fights with one punch, and I crossed the street anytime I saw them coming.

I didn't avoid all fights, though. I was arrested for a bar fight when I was about sixteen. As a teenager in Tarrytown, there were two bars you could drink in. The first, Cha Cha's, would have welcomed a baby if it had the balls to crawl in. Lynyrd Skynyrd played in a loop on the jukebox, and stacks of quarters lined the edges of the pool table, claiming next game. Getting served there for the first time felt like losing my indoor drinking virginity. No longer relegated to getting drunk in the freezing cold, I was exchanging money for booze without shame or fear. It was the beginning of the end. Chain-smoking Marlboros between shots of Jameson and pitchers of (always) Budweiser, I could not imagine a heaven that could match this roach-infested pit that reeked of vomit and spilled drinks. On weekends, teenagers jammed in and the parking lot seemed to have at least two people in every car—either smoking a joint or trying to have sex before or after smoking a joint. A ban from Cha Cha's for fighting or vomiting was a disgrace on many levels. It also meant walking across the street to the other bar that would serve any kid enterprising enough to buy a fake ID in a Times Square porn shop.

The Tarry Lounge was run by an older Irish gentleman, Joe McGrath, who was absolutely thrilled when we'd come in. The standard "third drink is on the house" policy at Cha Cha's was put to shame by Joe matching you drink for drink. The jukebox pumped out sentimental Clancy Brothers songs about sons lost to "the Troubles," but the place was clean and hospitable. At the end of the night, Joe would even go the extra mile, inviting us upstairs to his place to sleep off our drunk. We never went up there, but the possibility that we one day would kept his hope alive and the pitchers flowing.

Late one night at the Tarry Lounge, a three-way fight broke out. My friend Brian and I scrapped with a grown man named Eddie Russo. He pulled a switchblade *comb* on us. The fight spilled into the street, where we were arrested immediately, since the police station was fifty feet away. The next morning, my friend Johnny Trouble's mom bailed us out. I asked her recently what she remembered about that day and she said, "I remember wrapping up quarters for bail money—I needed $50. I ran out of wrappers, so I substituted aluminum foil to wrap the rest of the quarters. So, here I am at headquarters, paper and aluminum wrapped quarters in tow to bail you out. The Sergeant at the desk (a good guy) laughed so hard before informing me that he could not accept coins as bail money, so I headed to the local bank nearby to cash the coins into bills."

When my mother saw me walk into the house that afternoon, she figured that I'd gone out earlier that morning, when in fact, the night before I'd gone out through my window—a standard move on the weekends. It was not until the next day that she found out the real story in the paper.

I dodged a bullet not long after that when I was arrested for DUI and called my "parents" to come bail me out.

This photo was taken shortly after my brother and sister dressed up like my parents and bailed me out of jail for a DUI. The cops could not have cared less how ridiculous my brother and sister looked. They just wanted me out of their police station.

This was one of the many great examples that I presented to my little sister. Because she is three and a half years younger than I am, I had a pretty significant influence on Deirdre's life. I probably gave her her first drink and her first joint, and because of me, she hung out with a lot of people much older than she was. I wish I could say that I handled this in a more responsible way, but the truth is that I never really worried about Deirdre. She could fit in anywhere, and everybody loved her.

Over at Knollwood Country Club, I had worked my way to the top of the valet parking attendant ladder. As head PA, I got to make the schedule and call the shots. On Mondays and Tuesdays, very often there would be an outside outing at the country club. On this particular Tuesday, it was the Paper Tigers. This was a wealthy group of Japanese businessmen who loved to golf, so they spent a lot of money for this tournament every year. On that same Tuesday, however, my fellow parking attendant "Sneaky" Sean Carney and I had been invited to the shotgun wedding of a Guido waiter who also worked at the club. He was distressed about getting married and anxious that so few people would be attending his and his fiancée's wedding/springboard into marital failure.

Sean and I felt badly, so we grabbed two waitresses from the club, Susan and Cheryl, and headed to the church for the ceremony. The assistant manager of the club was a character named Ted Cotter. He looked like the director John Waters, with a pencil-thin moustache and a closeted gay persona that allowed Sean and I to charm him and get away with murder. Murder on this day involved not returning to the club following the wedding ceremony as we had promised Ted Cotter we would do. Instead we let the Guido waiter's father convince us to come back to the house in Yonkers to have just one glass of champagne.

Three hours later, we realized we should probably get back to Knollwood, as the Paper Tigers outing had started about an hour earlier. Our return was hampered by the line of cars backed up for a half mile in the driveway to the country club. Angry Japanese men stood next to their cars, wondering what they should do. (Japanese men tend not to think that quickly on their feet when it comes to a breakdown in the system.) Ted Cotter, dressed in his usual sleek sharkskin business suit, was now sweating profusely as he and Willie the shoe-shine guy jockeyed cars down to the parking lot.

We made our way into the club by entering through the exit. Sean was driving with Cheryl in the front, while I tended to Susan, who lay prone in the backseat of the convertible with her legs hanging over the side while vomiting into a plastic bag. As we were all drunk, an immediate firing was in order. But in this case, we were indispensable, and so as Sean and I began parking the cars—committing a separate act of DWI with each trip down the hill—Susan and Cheryl headed into the dining room to hustle out hors d'oeuvres and prepare for dinner. At one point, I heard a very loud crash: Susan had foolishly attempted to descend the stairs to the kitchen with a full tray. She did not make it. At the end of the day, we were called into Ted Cotter's office and given two-week suspensions. Willy Galloway also demanded that we turn over half of our tips since he had parked so many of the cars. Better that than the cattle prod.

Another parking-attendant incident happened during my people's holiday. Spring came early to Knollwood Country Club one year, and I was asked to park cars on the weekend of Saint Patrick's Day. Instead of the required black-and-white uniform, I arrived for work dressed in a green shirt with my face

Me with the 1983 cast of *Jersey Shore*.

painted green. This all seemed perfectly appropriate to me, and Knollwood was so laid back, I assumed the membership would be fine with it as well. One member was not. That member was Bob Fitzsimmons. When he pulled up in the afternoon trying to get in a few holes, he turned red with anger at seeing me dressed up like a fool at his country club. This didn't compute with me. I didn't really understand where the line was between having fun and working at a job. I saw that my father felt vulnerable as a member of the club to have his son working there. When he quietly ordered me to clean up, change, and get back to the job, I was confused. I'd assumed that the fun-loving, rebellious, Irish Bob Fitzsimmons would have gotten a kick out of this. But the Bronx kid who did well and joined a country club was not amused at all.

One night, soon after this, I found my dad equally unamused with me. I came in drunk and received a pretty solid beating. This did not stop me from my normal routine of sneaking back out the window to go get even drunker. Unfortunately, I was less agile than usual that night, and my parents heard the noise on the roof. Suddenly, they were standing beneath me saying, "Greg, get off the roof, you're drunk!" If there is normally a fight-or-flight response to danger, that night I introduced a third option. Scramble over the top of the roof, dive onto the front lawn, roll, and then run off into the darkness.

The next day, I woke up with a real dilemma. If I went home, it meant facing the balance of the punishment I had earned the night before. I decided to run away. Not a lot of emphasis on the word *away*, and very little on the word *run*. I stayed on my buddy Brian's couch for three days, not thinking at the time that his mother would, of course, call my parents to tell them I was okay.

Brian, now splitting his high school curriculum with classes in culinary school, was a regular partner in crime. His single mom worked overtime at a hospital, and his apartment became a home away from home for a lot of us. His mother was a saint who not only put up with half a dozen teenagers a day slumming in her apartment, she got most of us part-time jobs working in the hospital. With no kitchen jobs available, she offered me a position no male had ever filled in the history of the hospital: tray girl. I delivered meals to patients, being careful to wear a mask and gloves when interacting with the ones marked *biohazard*. One particularly sunny afternoon, Celine Hebble wished *not* to perform her duties alongside me at Phelps. She could not call in sick, having already worn out that card, so instead she played the next logical one: call in a bomb scare. The patients were almost evacuated before hospital security cracked the case.

Brian once convinced me to bake gingerbread houses with him. We then

took the freshly baked houses door-to-door, assuring the neighbors that the money was going to the Children's Hospital. One of these jaded folks called the police to investigate. Their hunch was right: the money was not going to Phelps Memorial Children's Wing. It was going to Andre Davis, who sold half ounces of marijuana for $60.

One of my first jobs was working for Andre. He was the blackest person I've ever seen in my life. He shone. I briefly sold weed for Andre. One day, I owed Andre money, so he dropped by my house. I walked into my upper-middle-class home to find my mother sitting in the living room having a cup of chamomile tea with Andre, the local drug dealer. Soon afterward, I terminated our professional relationship. But my mom really liked him. She still asks about him once in a while. "Where's Andre these days, honey? He was such a nice boy." Sing Sing, Mom.

During my "runaway" I was very sad, and on the evening I returned home, I stood in the backyard for a long time watching my mother read the newspaper on the couch in the warm light of our living room. It seemed so perfect, and yet I was running away from it. I went inside, my desire to be part of this world stronger than my fear of what might happen in my immediate future. Turns out, nothing really did happen.

That is what was so odd about my parents. The penal code was inconsistent, and what might get you smacked around one day could produce laughter the next. Apathy was the cruelest. There were times when my parents would ignore me for weeks after a stunt like this one. Not a word; we would pass in the hall like strangers except for the directives about when to be home and what needed to be done around the house. It's a reaction that I fight very hard not to inflict on anybody in my life now because I know how insignificant it made me feel.

I fight a lot of impulses as as adult—with mixed success. As of the writing of this book, I have never hit either of my children. I'm almost sure I never will. Please do not tell them this, or I will lose any guise of being in charge. Also, this feels very much like a violation of everything Irish people stand for. I'm not sure if the violence began with priests hitting kids or if the priests were trying to keep things consistent with what the kids got at home. My mother administered basic spankings and slaps to the head when we were young. Almost to the point where you could anticipate it coming, like the six o'clock news. As we became adolescents, we were upgraded to the belt. But when we grew to the same size as my mother and were able to block her strikes with a grin on our faces, Mom farmed jobs out to Dad. There is nothing more anxiety-provoking than a child's anticipation of a beating. It felt like a betrayal by my mother because most of the time it seemed like our family was unified against my father's temper. But now one of the members was selling one, or two, or all three of the other members out to the enemy. A dime-store shrink would make a meal out of this and the repercussions it may have had on my feeling safe in relationships with women. Fortunately, I don't consult dime-store shrinks. I go to high-end Beverly Hills psychiatrists who charge $200 an hour and blame only me.

Violence was just built into the system.

I remember one Christmas at my Uncle Gerry's house on Long Island when the cousins all started a food fight. Uncle Gerry marched into the room, picked up cousin Kevin by the ear, and dragged him into the bedroom. Our laughter only intensified as we heard what sounded like two pairs of boots tumbling in a clothes dryer. Gerry eventually returned to the adult table, and after five solemn minutes, we heard the rhythmic sound of Kevin banging his head against his bedroom wall. *Boom!* . . . *Boom!* . . . "Nobody loves me!" . . . *Boom!* . . . *Boom!* . . . "Nobody loves me!" This brought the laughter to an even higher pitch. Some people might read this passage and find it sad or even disturbing. It still puts a smile on my face.

I was not one of those kids who got caught a lot. I got in *trouble* a lot, but it was usually just due to bad luck, not stupidity. One night, in the middle of dinner, my father asked me how school had been the day before. I sat there with a sunburn, looking confused. "You know, the usual . . ."

"Learn anything good?"

"No. Why do you ask?"

He pulled out the front page of the *New York Times* sports section and then my parents laughed so hard I honestly think they wet their pants. They seemed to like me enough to overlook the fact that I was failing out of

The New York Times

Gary Hallberg, the first-round leader with a 67, hitting a shot from the rough on the third hole yesterday in the Manufacturers Hanover Westchester Classic.

That's me on the far right watching Gary Hallberg hit out of the rough at the Westchester Classic. I thought I'd be in the rough for skipping school that day, but my parents liked to keep things consistent.

school and in trouble almost constantly. It felt really bad to be struggling so much.

Eventually my father bought a vacation house for us in Port Saint Lucie, Florida. My dad's friend had died, so my father bought the house from his widow. We would go down there once a year, and my father believed that he had bought a good investment property. Twelve years later he would sell it at a loss. Almost immediately after the sale, Club Med built a resort there near where the New York Mets would set up their spring training camp soon after. I've tracked articles since then about how Port Saint Lucie has had the fastest-growing home prices in the country. When I told my friends at Rye Country Day that we had bought a second house in Florida, they were unimpressed because it was not Palm Beach. When I told my friends in Tarrytown that we had bought a house in Florida, they were sad and asked me when my family was moving. Gosh, poor people can be really dumb sometimes.

Moving between private school and the insanity of Tarrytown was difficult. One day, a kid from Rye Country Day named Teddy came to Tarrytown to hang out. An hour later he was running through the woods with me and another guy after we'd shot out the window of a moving car with a slingshot. Four Puerto Rican guys were chasing us as a pregnant woman sat in the passenger seat still shaking from the window next to her head having been blown out. Teddy had an asthma attack and fell to all fours. My friend Sean took off like a rabbit through the woods, and I stopped to help Teddy, knowing that I was giving my life for this wheezy douche.

The four guys reached us, grabbed us, and said they were taking us to the police. I'd never been so relieved in my life to visit the police. The detective in Tarrytown in charge of teenage assholes like myself was a guy named Detective Reggiano. His thin moustache, pockmarked face, and aviator glasses gave away his secret desire to be a 1970s homicide detective. After I had counseled Teddy not to say there was a third guy and to deny we had shot the window out, he immediately ratted out Sean and told Detective Reggiano where we had thrown the slingshot. What an asshole.

It wasn't Teddy's fault he came from a family of assholes. They belonged to three country clubs and they were assholes. Teddy invited me to his family's house in Palm Beach one winter while my family was down in Florida for winter break. My family dropped me off in front of a mile-long driveway leading up to a mansion. Their jaws were wide open. Teddy came shuffling out in penny loafers, holding a lacrosse stick. He casually told me that his parents had some friends visiting and I couldn't come in. I thought my dad was going to get a gun and murder every occupant of the mansion. We were humiliated. And they were assholes.

Detective Reggiano and I became familiar with each other through a lot of juvenile delinquency charges. I don't know what my $200-an-hour therapist would say about vandalism, but it felt really good back then. I'm embarrassed to say that we would break windows at Marymount College, and break into homes that were not occupied. We'd go anywhere we could hang out and party—anywhere we could escape boredom.

Uncompleted homework assignments started piling up, and I developed a reputation among the teachers for being difficult. Rye Country Day was far more patient with me than I ever really deserved, and I think often of several teachers that changed my life by not giving up on me.

Dear Mrs. Fitzsimmons

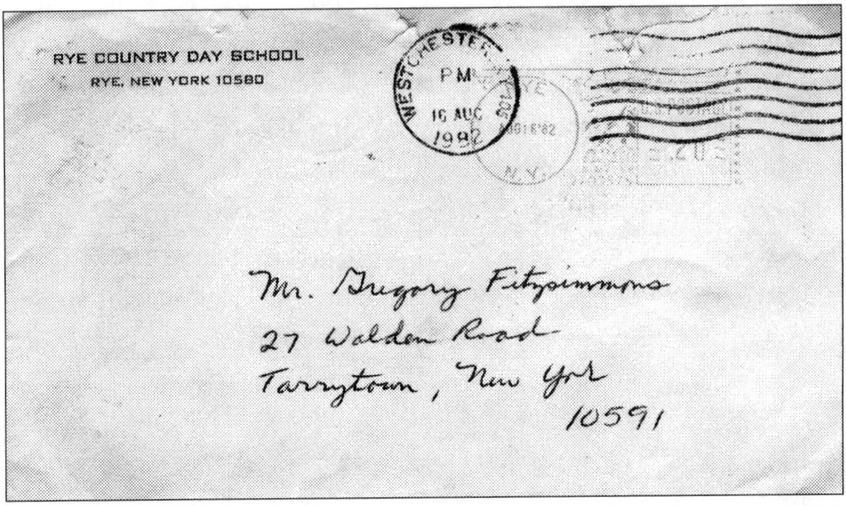

RYE COUNTRY DAY SCHOOL
RYE, NEW YORK 10580
WESTCHESTER
PM
16 AUG
1982
Mr. Gregory Fitzsimmons
27 Walden Road
Tarrytown, New York
10591

RYE COUNTRY DAY SCHOOL

Gregory Fitzsimmons — STUDENT

Advisor Comment — COURSE

2/11/82 — DATE

12 11 (10) 9 — GRADE

MARK

While Greg's grades have improved since last year, there was a drop in three of his five courses at the end of the first semester. Even more disconcerting are the continuing reports of misbehavior and rudeness in and out of class. He seems headed for failure in French I. To receive an R.C.D.S. diploma, he must successfully pass three years of a language. He clearly cannot afford to fail but I detect only minimum concern on his part. Whenever I discuss these problems with him he presents a picture of someone who can't understand what all the fuss is about. I do feel that he has made some legitimate arguments on his own behalf. However, the tide is going against him and he may well find himself in another school next year. Mostly, he will have himself to blame.

Sincerely,

Richard Braun

ADVISOR

SIGNATURE

By senior year, I had pot for lunch most days:

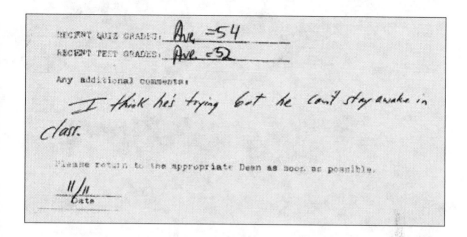

Having failed to make the boys' baseball team for three consecutive years, I decided to shift my focus. I did what any hot-blooded, rebellious boy in high school would do: I founded a golf team.

For some reason, despite being in the middle of some of the best courses in the country, Rye had no golf team. I spoke to someone from the administration who introduced me to an alumnus then belonging to Westchester Country Club. Randall was a great man who I believe inherited $10 million and had no aspirations in life besides creating a championship golf team for Rye Country Day School. He outfitted eleven of us with intense yellow cashmere sweaters, blue polyester slacks, and golf bags. Every afternoon he would shuttle us from the school to what is considered one of the top golf courses in the world. Westchester Country Club is home to the Westchester Classic and the U.S. Open.

RCDS's new team had a thirst not just for winning but also for rum. I kept a bottle of rum in my golf bag unbeknownst to Randall. He generously bought us Cokes for our nine-hole practice round, which we mixed with the rum on the second tee.

The party on the course became infamous and soon dozens of kids were trying out for the team. One afternoon, three varsity baseball players were busted for missing practice so they could hang with us on the golf course. Our first year in the league, we not only outdrank every other team, we

One of the most feared gangs in Westchester.

Captain Greg Fitzsimmons demonstrates his championship golf swing.

Golf Captures League Title

by Rick Lipsey

What glows in the dark, melts in the sun, and travels in Cadillacs? Yes, the 1984 varsity golf squad. With their vibrant sweaters and finely trimmed slacks, the '84 linksters have not only established themselves with society, but have also captured their first ever Fairchester League Golf Championship. They compiled an 8-1 record, marred only by an eleven stroke loss to power "Club" house Iona Prep.

The Cats were a solid team with six players consistently shooting below 47, for nine holes. The first three positions were held by Danny "Helicopter" Milberg, Jim "I hit it well, but..." Lowy, and Rick "Luscious" Lipsey. These three players had excellent seasons, winning all but three of their matches. Milberg broke a team record set way back in 1804 by shooting a blazing 34 at

Cont'd p.2

Golf

Cont'd from p.1

Westchester Country Club, while Lipsey and Lowy enjoyed steady seasons.

The final three positions were filled by senior captain Greg Fitzsimmons, Pete Weissman, and Brandt Enos. Also seeing action this season were Angelo "Dr. Hook" Fazio, Scott Shea, Gary Norman, and Neal Ruskin.

The Cats were simply the class of R.C.D.S. They not only outdressed everyone else, but they were the only undefeated, untied boys varsity squad in league play this year in the school. They demolished every league opponent except for Brunswick, who played valiantly, but fell to the mighty Cats by a single stroke.

Not only did the squad go undefeated in league play, but they also ran away with the League Championship Tournament at lush Yale Golf Club. Rick Lipsey carded a ten over par 80 to place second, and he was joined by Jim Lowy, 83, and "Helicopter" Milberg, 86, in making the All-League team. Greg Fitzsimmons recorded a 90 to round out the championship team.

failed to lose a single match. We won the league championship, and the team continues on to this day—although my guess is those kids are coming up a little short in the alcohol department. I'm going to have to go back there and look into it.

Meanwhile, back in academia, I was winning no championships.

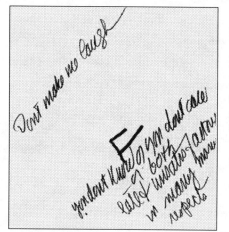

This grade and comment came from Dr. Bocchius on a tenth-grade history essay. I pray to God that he has not since become a book reviewer.

On the other hand, I found my creative writing teacher, Mr. Jones, to be a visionary.

ROMEO & JULIET

IIii??

Greg Fitzsimmons
EN364
2-10-88

95

Creative writing class was the only subject in which I put forth any effort. This was encouraged by an amazing teacher named Morrow Jones. I wrote humorous essays rather than book reports, and he thought it was great. When he wrote that I might consider writing comedy for a living, something clicked in me and a seed was planted.

Morrow was married to a hippie librarian at the school and he always reminded me of Donald Sutherland playing the professor who lectured about opening your mind with marijuana in the movie *Animal House.* He laughed at the comments I made in class and seemed to have a much longer fuse than most of my other teachers. He even bought me a tuxedo for the prom after I'd told him I thought it would be stupid. It was a vintage 1948 double-breasted tuxedo made in Brussels that he'd spotted in a thrift store one day. His encouragement would never be forgotten and opened me up to the possibility that comedy could be something used not just for evil.

My buddy Marlo and I used to go into the comedy clubs in Greenwich Village on the weekends. We were obsessed with stand-up comedy. At that time, the regular comics working the clubs were guys like Rick Overton and Richard Belzer. Marlo and I liked to sit up front, and—I cringe to think about this now—we heckled the performers. We weren't trying to be destructive, we were trying to be part of the show. I can remember sitting at a table listening to these great comics as I scrambled in my mind to come up with ideas to throw in.

On the drive home, Marlo and I regaled each other with the great moments that we had added to the show. We often hung around outside the club afterward to try to talk to the comedians. When one of them was nice enough to give us a few minutes of his or her time, we felt like the coolest kids on the planet. Bill Grundfest was a regular at the Comedy Cellar, along with Rick Chrome on piano. Both were always very cool to us, and looking back, I appreciate it even more now knowing that we were probably the two most annoying assholes in the city.

A few weeks before I miraculously graduated, we had a high school talent show, and I signed up. Before the show, Marlo and I laughed at the absurdity of the principal warning me not to be inappropriate. We were laughing because we were in the preschool playground snorting lines off the slide.

Once onstage, I went straight into a bit about the secret sexual relationship between my Western Civilizations teacher and my very hot art teacher. The kids were dying, and I was on top of the world. It was like a dream. Then my microphone went dead. I saw the principal on the side of the stage, smiling, with the cord in his hand. After a few moments of confusion, I began screaming the rest of my act to the auditorium. And I was back in charge just like that. I was doing what I had always done, but now an audience was laughing. I could not be stopped. The principal looked so powerless. Suddenly everything was flipped upside down.

I'd dreamt about doing stand-up my entire life, and it was everything I thought it would be. Afterward, I walked outside, and I screamed with joy. I was hooked. As it turned out, I would not go onstage again for years, but I thought about little else. Committing to being a comedian was still years off for me. I had a lot more demons to work through before I was mature enough for a life of telling dick jokes to drunks and hitting on waitresses for a living. I graduated by some miracle, not knowing what I would do next. I only knew that I wouldn't be going to college.

Me and Marlo, arm in arm. Which means one of us just told the other he had coke.

Europe on Nine Beers a Day

College was the furthest thing from my mind. I was just relieved that I had squeaked through high school. But if I was going to live at home, my parents were not going to tolerate me doing nothing. So I worked at night as a cook in a T.G.I. Friday's and parked cars during the day. I saved up $3,000 and took off on a six-month trip backpacking around Europe.

Saying good-bye before going to Europe for six months.

I didn't know what I wanted to do with my life, but I knew I wouldn't have time like this again, so I wanted to take advantage of it. Looking back, it was the best thing I could have possibly done. It opened my eyes to the ways that other people lived, but it was also a wake-up call that living on your own with no real job skills or education was a shitload of work. This was the first step toward what would later emerge as self-confidence—something I'd only heard about before and apparently has something to do with going out on your own.

Taking care of myself was a lot harder than I thought it would be, and I was homesick. I especially missed my sister, who was now living alone with my parents and whose friendship I had become used to having all the time. As corny as this might sound, the Elton John song "Daniel" still makes me tear up a little bit. We wrote a lot of letters back and forth when I was away. I know my parents were worried, but they were also very proud of me. The whole time I was away, I felt like I was proving something to them and to myself. One of the real bright spots came in Denmark when a model named Susanne had sex with me. Then she did again. She had sex with me twice. She was a model. From Denmark. She then wrote to me while I was in Spain on the second half of my trip asking for me to help her move to the United States.

> great if you can do something for
> me.
> I don't naw ob I came to naw-york
> fist I must have a job, and then
> I came to New-York for 3 week's in july
> to visit you and your famili. It will
> be great. You see I would not leave
> before I knew something to come home
> to (work) you see it's about the
> money. I don't have enough money

Not connecting the sex to the request for a green card, I immediately petitioned my parents to sponsor her move to the U.S.—like you would for a starving child, only in this case it would be a Scandinavian model with whom I would have sex.

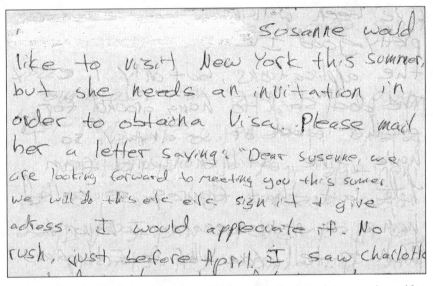

Sosanne would like to visit New York this summer, but she needs an invitation in order to obtain a visa. Please mail her a letter saying: "Dear Susanne, we are looking forward to meeting you this summer we will do this etc etc. sign it + give adress. I would appreciate it. No rush, just before April. I saw charlotte

My parents never replied to my request. I could be twenty-five years into a marriage with a woman who barely speaks English right now if they had just . . .

They were able to track my entire trip through letters they received. I sent long, detailed letters weekly. In one, I describe hitchhiking across Ireland when a guy picked me up and soon thereafter offered me "Poteen," which is Irish moonshine. (No, this is not the part of the book where I am raped.) I had one capful and almost coughed my asshole out of my mouth. He chugged it like it was water, and then we stopped for a cup of soup. He immediately passed out at the counter, so I had to lug him back to his truck and then drive it all the way to Galway on the wrong side of the road. When I got to the city line, the guy suddenly woke up refreshed and we started making quick stops at houses around town. "Wait a minute! You're a bootlegger and only picked me up as a cover! Awesome!"

My very next ride was from a sophisticated woman who turned out to be the mayor of Galway. She invited me to a fancy hotel for "an American

Thanksgiving dinner" and I was treated like an honored guest. I didn't have the heart to tell the mayor that I was a bootlegger. She delivered something to my parents that was foreign to them on many levels: a letter of *praise.*

While in Ireland, I also rented a house for a month in the town my grandfather Florence was from (Kenmare, in County Kerry). I wrote more than I've ever written in my life and felt very connected to the smart but tough people from the town. I'd walk to the Atlantic Pub every evening and have pints with the barmaid, Molly, who I quickly fell for. At night I fed peat (which is dry dirt) into the fireplace to try to warm the old farmhouse, and I think it rained every day I was there. I loved it. I'd sometimes pull out a creased, old, Irish five-pound bill that my mother had put in my hand when

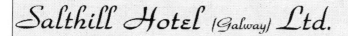

Salthill Hotel (Galway) *Ltd.*

Telephones: (091) 22711
            22115

PROMENADE,
SALTHILL,
GALWAY,
IRELAND.

23rd. November, 1984

Dear Mr. and Fitzsimmons,

Yesterday, being Thanksgiving Day, we had the pleasure of having your son Greg, at the dinner and party which we hold in the Hotel every year.

Considering it is always a bit of a worry when boys or girls leave home,(for their parents), I decided to let you know, that you have got a very nice boy, and all the people were very impressed with his good manners, and his ability to mix so well with older people. I think he enjoyed the evening, as I am sure he felt lonely being away from his family. He seems to be having an enjoyable trip.

I also gave him the address of my niece and husband in Northern Ireland, should he decide to go there. It is always good to have a contact.

I hope you had a Happy Thanksgiving. We had a good party here.

Yours sincerely,
(Mrs) Margaret Murray.

In the current Irish economy, this has the same value as a yellow Post-it note.

I left for my trip. She told me it had been given to her by her parents twenty years earlier so she could spend it on something special during her honeymoon there. Instead she held on to it and passed it on to me so I could spend it on something special.

I never got around to spending that bill. Years ago, I hid it away in my sock drawer and some day will pass it on to one of my kids. Or, quite possibly, the maid has already stolen it and mailed it back to her family in Guatemala.

I met up with a Cork man named Theo (pronounced "T-O") who was a cousin of a friend from New York. After a couple of weeks dragging me through the hard-drinking pubs of Cork City, he took a break from college to hitch around the west coast with me. Some of the best times in my life. One morning we woke up in a bed-and-breakfast in Ireland's answer to Newark, New Jersey: Macroom. The keeper was not amused by our returning the night before in the wee hours, and so she roused us at seven o'clock for the standard overcooked eggs with several mystery pig parts fried and served beside tough brown bread. When she padded into the kitchen to retrieve more lukewarm tea, Theo placed a large sausage in the crotch of her thermal underpants, which were draped over the hissing radiator. Once caught, we were thrown out, laughing our way out to the curb with our thumbs pleading for a ride out of this nightmare. By the time someone pulled over, we had both thrown up on the side of the road.

I wrote about adventures in letters home and, thankfully, received just as many back at post offices mapped out in my itinerary. Being away from my family for the first time, I began really appreciating the fun we'd always shared. Feeling more like an adult, I was beginning to have the ability to accept my parents more. Their letters contained photos reminding me of the great times I seemed to have forgotten about.

While traveling was exciting and challenging, I wasn't used to feeling like an outsider. The more I observed people in other cultures, the more I grasped how insane my own family and friends were. I found most Europeans lacking in the blind rage toward random things that I so enjoyed back in

Theo and I founded an alcoholic wing of the Boy Scouts.

the States. (I believe the last incident of road rage over there was in Rome and it involved chariots.)

Europe is filled with very serious and academic people. In German youth hostels, they wake you at the crack of dawn, make you clean up your room, and then kick you out at 7 a.m. One night I slept in a park after being locked out because I'd returned after midnight.

These letters and pictures brought back the absurd laughter we'd shared daily and I remember the embarrassment of feeling homesick when I was now completely free from my parents' control. This acute loneliness was subdued by high quality beer and sexual relations with women from other countries. The only fight I remember having was on a train in France when a Moroccan dude tried to steal my backpack.

Being away offered me perspective on the world I'd grown up in and allowed me to believe in myself more than I ever had in the past as a poor student, bad athlete, and intimidated son.

This one documents the very large minifridge bill accrued from nightly chambermaid visits where we were offered turndown service. (Who could turn that down?)

This valuable photograph captures the rarely seen "bringing the dish to the sink" only rumored to occur in the wild.

I bet you were thinking he must have let me win sometimes to make me feel good. That's a bet you just lost.

Mom and I Greco-Roman wrestling. I bet you were thinking I let her win. (You're a pretty bad gambler, aren't you?)

Back then it wasn't called drinking and driving. Just driving.

By July I'd spent literally *all* of my money and doctored the expiration date on my train pass so many times that it resembled a buried treasure map; it was time to head home. Fortunately, when I had still had money a month earlier, I'd purchased a concert ticket from a fellow traveler in Greece. It was for the night before I was to fly home from London. Europe provided me with a parting gift so incredible, I still can't believe that it happened. Springsteen was closing out his *Born in the U.S.A.* tour in Wembley Stadium on the Fourth of July. You've got to be shitting me!

I had eaten so little that I felt dizzy most of the show, but I stayed through the four-and-a-half-hour religious experience before taking the underground tube to Heathrow Airport.

When I returned to New York, my father congratulated me on getting into Boston University—which was an amazing feat, seeing as I had never applied to Boston University. Turns out that while I was away, my dad applied for me. He must have written one hell of an essay.

We took a vacation in the Poconos. I wasn't thinking at the time that we were all probably at our peaks. I guess you never really are aware of things like that until later.

With a month to go before heading off to college, I partied a lot in Tarrytown. Things seemed a little bit less exciting and a lot sadder. So many kids from my town died from drinking-related accidents I couldn't even keep track. When I look back, I see how I could have been one of them, but I wasn't. Somehow, throughout my life I've managed to go to the edge without falling off. I came extremely close one night that summer when my brother, my buddy Tommy, and I went to a bar in the next town over. Some feathers were ruffled on the dance floor when we told this brain-dead townie that he shouldn't have his three-year-old daughter in a bar at two in the morning. The guy later followed us out to the parking lot. I said something to him, and he dived into the open side window of our car. After about thirty seconds of pounding the guy's head with elbows and knees, the V-8 Buick Riviera was cruising at around thirty miles per hour. Seemed like it was time to say goodbye to our new friend. We threw the guy out the

My dad with his longtime agent, Don Buchwald.

passenger window and all I can remember is seeing him tumbling end over end on the pavement.

This would have been an excellent moment to start making our way home. But something familiar happened: I kind of snapped. Turning the car around despite the screaming protests of the other passengers, I tried to run the guy over. (I know—what the fuck?!) Luckily, he got out of the way, but we were now facing the wrong way on a one-way street. By the time I headed back out, the guy was by the side of the road and threw a brick into the windshield. We were chased through the town by a bunch of the guy's friends who were in a pickup truck. Halfway home, Tommy told me to let him out of the car. He thought I was insane and said he'd rather walk home.

Whatever longing I had during high school to be around Tarrytown was fading as I saw what the real possibilities were. In the fall, I headed out and never moved back.

Disciplinary Reports:
The Building Blocks to Success

> Rarely are sons similar to their fathers; most are worse, and a
> few are better.
>
> —Homer, *The Odyssey*

I packed a duffel bag, and my dad drove me up to college. Pulling into Boston, I was giddy as I witnessed 250,000 students moving into apartments and dorms around the many colleges throughout the city. But what really sold me on the town was the history. This was the city that had thrown its tea in the harbor and told the Brits to go fuck themselves. It felt like a place I might fit in nicely.

This would turn out to be yet another step toward that confidence that was now building in me. My dad was proud because he had attended BU for

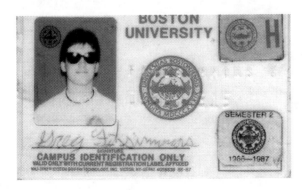

I wore sunglasses because I forgot to wear my shirt that said COCKY ASSHOLE.

two years in 1959 but hadn't finished getting his bachelor's degree. His tour of the city made it obvious why. He could name every bar on Commonwealth Avenue but seemed at a loss when I asked him where the classrooms were. I took to the city instantly, as my father had twenty-five years before. The connection was akin to what I'd experienced in Ireland the year before, only the friendly, trusting attitude was gone. In its place was a hostile cynicism that left me feeling almost constantly like I was about to be punched in the face. This was not neurosis: people were randomly punched in the face all the time. You could be cheering for the wrong team at Boston Garden, checking out a girl whose boyfriend was nearby, or, God forbid, wearing an article of clothing not bought at an army and navy store and therefore making you a "fag." Three guys in a 1978 Monte Carlo once jumped me because I didn't dive out of the pedestrian crosswalk fast enough when they came barreling through it.

Anyway, things started off pretty well until the night I was charged with assault with a deadly weapon. Let me explain . . .

Stumbling home from a series of keg parties one night, my friend Jeff and I found that a girl we knew from our dorm had been sexually attacked. She described the assailant, and Jeff and I split up to look for him.

With my stellar luck, I came across the two guys—one of whom matched the girl's description—he was wearing a South Lincoln Prep school sweatshirt. They were football players and tried to run, so I chased them into the lobby of an apartment building. I broke a glass Veryfine juice bottle and held them both at the security gate with the dangerous end of a kiwi-mango blend until they were arrested.

Here's where it gets really funny. The female victim of the alleged sexual assault then decided *not* to press charges because she was a freshman and didn't want to disrupt her year. This stroke of good fortune inspired the two jocks to charge me with assault with a deadly weapon. A meeting was set up between the girl, the jocks, the dean of housing, and me.

The dean was not looking like he was in my corner, having previously told me, "Boston University does not need any New York Rambos here."

Long story short: the girl threatened to press charges against the jocks, and the jocks, in turn, dropped the charges against me.

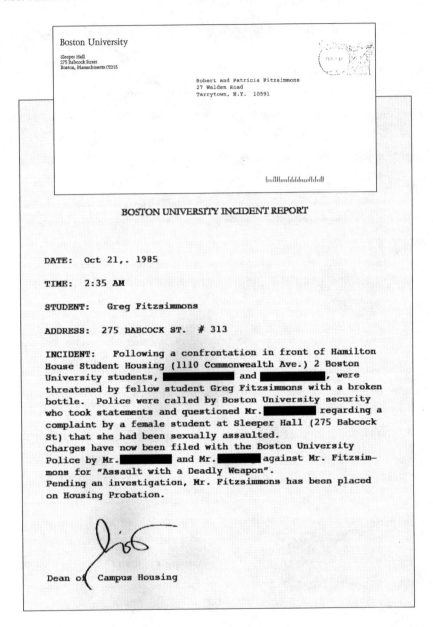

Boston University
Sleeper Hall
275 Babcock Street
Boston, Massachusetts 02215

Robert and Patricia Fitzsimmons
27 Walden Road
Tarrytown, N.Y. 10591

BOSTON UNIVERSITY INCIDENT REPORT

DATE: Oct 21,. 1985

TIME: 2:35 AM

STUDENT: Greg Fitzsimmons

ADDRESS: 275 BABCOCK ST. # 313

INCIDENT: Following a confrontation in front of Hamilton House Student Housing (1110 Commonwealth Ave.) 2 Boston University students, ▮▮▮▮ and ▮▮▮▮, were threatened by fellow student Greg Fitzsimmons with a broken bottle. Police were called by Boston University security who took statements and questioned Mr. ▮▮▮ regarding a complaint by a female student at Sleeper Hall (275 Babcock St) that she had been sexually assaulted.
Charges have now been filed with the Boston University Police by Mr. ▮▮▮ and Mr. ▮▮▮ against Mr. Fitzsimmons for "Assault with a Deadly Weapon".
Pending an investigation, Mr. Fitzsimmons has been placed on Housing Probation.

Dean of Campus Housing

I believe the BU football team was 2-11 that year.

Luckily, my little sister would snag most of these letters out of the mailbox, and my mom has never seen them! (Until this book comes out.)

Despite the usual anger management issues, I was focused on my studies with a confidence that grew from my travels as well as living in a large

Boston University

West Campus Residence Halls
275 Babcock Street
Boston, Massachusetts 02215
617/353-3902

February 3, 1986

Gregory Fitzsimmons
Sleeper Hall
Room 313

Dear Gregory,

On December 6th, 1985 a noise disturbance created via a water and shaving cream fight occurred on the third floor. You were warned by the R.A., that if another incident occurred you would receive a noise violation. It has been reported that you have been warned on numerous occasions but, you were given your final warning on December 6th.

On December 7th, 1985 you were issued a noise violation for carrying on a loud conversation in the elevator quad at 2:47a.m. When the R.A. came out to ask you to quiet down you became louder, verbally abusive, and you threatened the R.A. You were told that it would be in your best interest to go to your room. You not only refused this advise, you returned to the elevator quad approximately ten minutes later and continued to disturb the community. The next day you informed the R.A. that you were drunk and not responsible for your behavior and you apologized.

On December 10th, 1985 we met in my office to discuss these incidents. You did not deny any of the behavior described in the incident reports. You again apologized for threatening your R.A. stating that you were too drunk to know what you were doing. We discussed your excessive drinking which you shrugged off and did not feel was a problem. I explained that we did have the resources to respond if you ever decided you needed help but drinking is not an acceptable excuse for inappropriate behavior in the Residence Halls.

As a result of a noise violation, which, uncontested, would automatically require the sanction of Residence Hall Probation, and threating a staff member as well as ignoring your final warning for disturbing the community, I am forced to place you on Deferred Suspension. This involves the deferred imposition of a disciplinary suspension from the residence hall and is conditional upon your not committing an offense against residence hall regulations from now until December 31st, 1986.

Second semester, I settled down and merely repeatedly threatened my Resident Assistant (RA).

dormitory filled with naïve freshman who had almost no real-life experience. One kid, a sheep farmer from Ohio we named "Hick," learned a lot from that first year. He was nabbed by campus security while peeing in the dorm stairwell. We both ran, but he never gave me up, and served forty hours of community service for keeping his mouth shut. I owed him one.

I was beginning to replace my cycles of shame with a newfound cycle of confidence. While good grades were not yet making me feel intelligent, they did indicate to me (and my parents) that I was capable of working hard and not giving up. I do believe that college can be an enormous waste of time and money for some kids, but I was in the right place at the right time and getting everything out of it that I could.

Boston University

College of Basic Studies
871 Commonwealth Avenue
Boston, Massachusetts 02215

February 3, 1987

Mr. Greg Fitzsimmons
27 Walden Road
Tarrytown, NY 10591

Dear Greg:

I am extremely pleased to recognize your academic achievements during this past semester. Your attaining the Dean's List for the first semester of the 1986-87 academic year reflects your strong effort and seriousness of purpose in a very demanding and competitive program.

I congratulate you and wish you continued success.

Sincerely,

Brendan F. Gilbane
Dean

One of the most moronic traditions in the Western world is the pilgrimage of college students to beach towns during their spring break. The idea that you need to break up the nonstop partying of college with a week of even heavier drinking is perhaps at the root of why our nation seems to be slipping into last place among the educated of the world. That being said, when I was a freshman, there was a plan among about twenty of my friends to rent a Winnebago and head down to Fort Lauderdale, Florida, in March; and I was *in*, baby!

As the date approached, more and more guys bailed until we were reduced to six guys, one hotel room, and tickets for a thirty-six-hour ride (each way) on a Greyhound bus. The night before, I was the only one drunk enough to still think this was a good idea, so I went. By myself. Because those guys are a bunch of pussies!

I began the journey with a twelve-pack of Moosehead beer and as much dry food as I could sneak out of the dorm cafeteria. I shared my twelve-pack with a redhead from Boston College. By the time we were in Hartford, we were making out. That continued until she disembarked at the Port Authority Bus Terminal in New York. I said good-bye and promised I'd stay in touch. However, when I looked out the bus window and saw that she had an enormous ass, the relationship was over. By Pennsylvania, I was hung over and out of alcohol, which was fine because that's when six guys from Penn State boarded the bus with peach schnapps and cases of Budweiser. Spring break was back on! Hey, wait a minute—who stole my jacket? Never mind, who cares?!

Thirty-six hours of drinking while being pickpocketed by various transitory figures in the dark of the night is less exciting than one might think. With no hotel to stay in, I began wandering in and out of happy hours, sleeping on the floor of not just the Penn State guys' hotel rooms but those of drunken college students from all around the country. On my last day, I woke up on the beach, and by the time I got to my feet, I had third-degree burns on the back of my neck and legs. I don't know if I can explain the intense pain I experienced from sitting on a plastic Greyhound seat sweating through sunburn and a hangover on my way back to New York. Was it worth it? Fuck no, it was one of the worst weeks of my life. But at least I did it, not like those pussies back in Boston.

If you are one of the guys in this picture with me, I actually had a shitty week hanging out with you, so don't bother looking me up trying to "reconnect."

My fondest memory from freshman year was without a doubt when my dad took me to game four of the 1986 World Series at Fenway Park. Our family had been Mets fans my whole life. This meant we were losers. Year in and year out, we were ridiculed, but Dad's radio station carried the games, and he was friends with some of the players.

Then something unheard of happened. In the mid-eighties, the Mets began getting good. Really good. And by good, I don't mean that they were well-conditioned or well-behaved. They were the most outrageous team in baseball. Darryl Strawberry and Dwight Gooden had coke problems, and three players were arrested for a bar fight in Houston. But they started beating good teams.

In 1986 my family hung on every game of the historic National League playoffs against the Houston Astros, and suddenly our Mets faced the Boston Red Sox in the World Series. I sat in dorm rooms surrounded by "Massholes" until the Red Sox led the series two games to one. My dad called and told me he was heading up to Boston to take me to game four. The Mets won the game, and I can still remember saying good-bye to my Dad in the

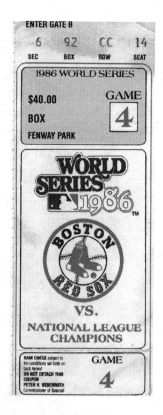

VIP club at Fenway with Rusty Staub, a buddy of my Dad's from his bar, Rusty's, in New York. I thought, as I had many times in my life, that I had the coolest dad in history.

Three nights later, I thought I was saying good-bye to the dream of a Mets world championship. The Red Sox led game six, 5–3, in the bottom of the tenth inning, needing just one more out to win the series. What followed was one of the greatest comebacks in baseball history: three singles, a wild pitch, and then the sad sight of Boston first baseman Bill Buckner letting Mookie Wilson's easy grounder sneak between his legs and into right field. Ray Knight scored from second as Shea Stadium erupted. New York went on to take game seven. The Mets were winners. We were winners. Felt weird.

I called my dad and we didn't even need to say much. He had brought me along on many wonderful rides in my life. The guy knew how to have fun and he taught me how to do it right.

I felt closer to my dad than I ever had, but there was a degree to which I couldn't really ever know him. I would send him letters sometimes that were very raw and honest. He never acknowledged getting any of them. (Cue the Jim Croce music.)

Stand-up comedy remained an obsession and I spent many nights in college hanging around the local clubs. Before this time I saw comedy as this amazing, powerful thing that made people laugh. I was never a snob about what type of comedy I liked, but I was drawn to comics who didn't pander to the crowd.

In Boston I was exposed to a new style of comedy altogether. The "I don't give a shit about you" attitude immediately struck a chord with me. I worshipped comedians like Don Gavin, Steve Sweeney, Kenny Rogerson, and others that most people have never heard of but whom I consider to be among the best ever. These comics belong in this city that claims Ted Williams, the greatest home run hitter of all time who refused to ever tip his hat to the cheering crowd. This city that claims Larry Bird, the greatest shooter in basketball who refused to do interviews or hire anybody to mow his lawn.

The voice of comedy in Boston grew out of a culture steeped in Catholic repression, racial tension, and the kind of jaded belligerence that can result

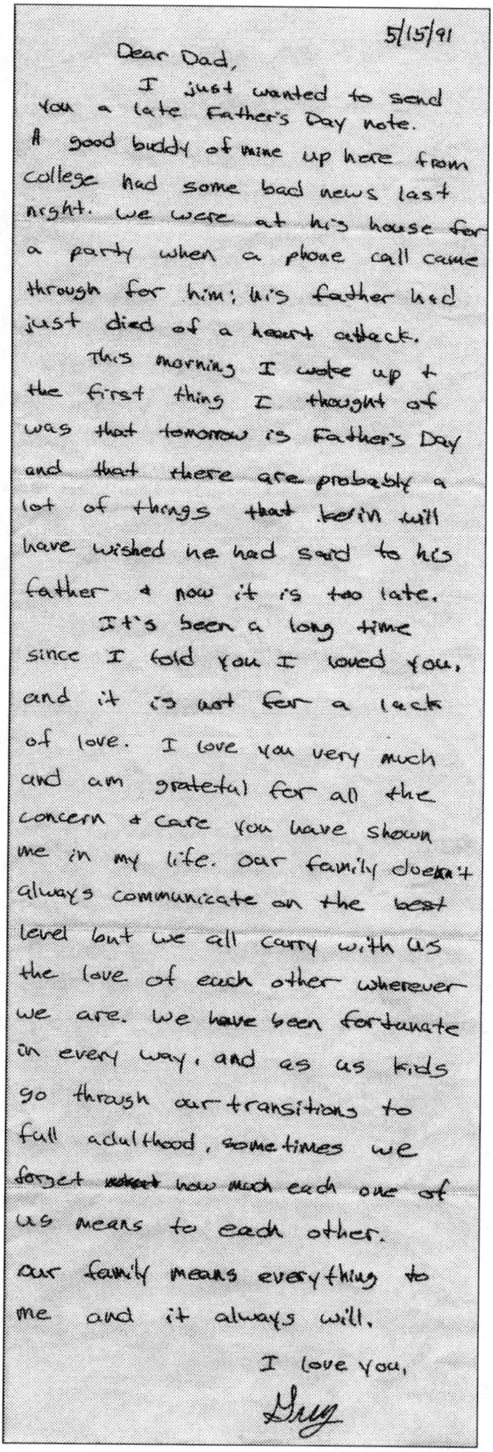

5/15/91

Dear Dad,

I just wanted to send you a late Father's Day note. A good buddy of mine up here from college had some bad news last night. We were at his house for a party when a phone call came through for him; his father had just died of a heart attack.

This morning I woke up + the first thing I thought of was that tomorrow is Father's Day and that there are probably a lot of things that Kevin will have wished he had said to his father & now it is too late.

It's been a long time since I told you I loved you, and it is not for a lack of love. I love you very much and am grateful for all the concern & care you have shown me in my life. Our family doesn't always communicate on the best level but we all carry with us the love of each other wherever we are. We have been fortunate in every way, and as us kids go through our transitions to full adulthood, sometimes we forget how much each one of us means to each other. Our family means everything to me and it always will.

I love you,

Guy

only from bone-chilling winters lasting five months. The tone of comedy at that time existed in a narrow window between silly antiauthoritarianism and wanting to punch you in the face. Here in Boston, the audience was given an opportunity to listen to somebody cooler, more successful, and funnier than they were, and they would be denied any say in the contents of the material.

I saw that the more a comedian backed off when an audience became uncomfortable, the more the show shifted from being about the comedian to being about the crowd. I saw guys like Mike Donovan craft jokes that started out with a gut punch followed by repeated kicks to the crotch until the audience was in a complete state of surrender. They're offended? Then go bigger. They're uncomfortable? Dial it up a notch. If you're lucky, they'll walk out of the room. In some cities, this would be grounds for immediate dismissal from a club. In Boston, it was like a badge of honor.

When I hear comedians talk about how much they love the crowd and just enjoy making people laugh, they are dead to me. I will never laugh at a comedian whose goal is reading and fulfilling the crowd's desires. I learned in Boston that a really good comedian takes no direction and instead controls the crowd with material he believes in and an attitude he has earned. Oh, yeah, and in most cases back then, a mullet.

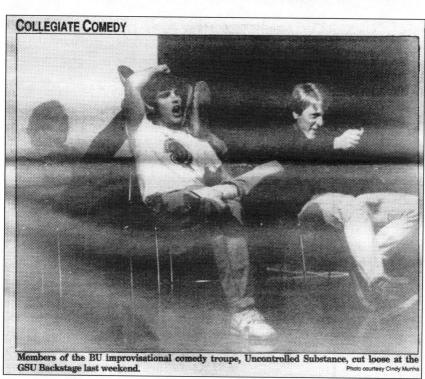

Members of the BU improvisational comedy troupe, Uncontrolled Substance, cut loose at the GSU Backstage last weekend. Photo courtesy Cindy Murtha

I was now testing the waters by doing an occasional open-mic night and later on joining an improv troupe called "Uncontrolled Substance" (because, you see, we couldn't not be controlled . . .).

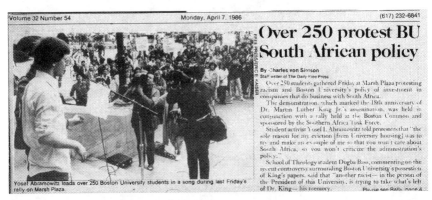

Me at a BU protest rally (from BU's newspaper). The speaker before the cameras is Yosef Abromowitz, who later married comedienne Sarah Silverman's sister.

Another less destructive way that I was channeling my energy then was getting involved with different protests on campus. At that time, they focused on BU's investments in apartheid, restrictions on overnight guests of the opposite sex in the dorms, and the right-wing policies of the school's president John Silber. BU students were wealthy and fairly entitled. It felt good getting involved with what was going on—through writing pieces in the school paper and attending demonstrations—and seeing that the student body could make a difference. I also found you could very often have sex with female protestors. Good, angry sex with undertones of real social change.

Throughout college, one of my part-time jobs was being a referee at ice hockey games. I'd played my whole life but had never been on the justice end of the game. It was tough because if you missed a call or made a bad one you were screamed at but had to keep your cool and stay in control. It may have been the first time in my life where I was the authority figure. I liked that feeling.

The most argumentative team was always BU Law School. They were in the middle of a very scrappy game with some fraternity when a fight broke out. Honoring standard hockey fight protocol, I allowed the fight to go on until the two players fell to the ice. That is when the ref steps in because it is much easier to handle and the players are generally exhausted by then. As I got between them, one of the players accidentally punched me in the face. I instantly snapped and started hitting him back and had to be pulled off of him by another ref. I was called to the athletic director's office and suspended from work for two weeks.

Returning home to New York during vacations was becoming less and less interesting. After my sophomore year in college, I was home for the summer, staring at race-car wallpaper while reading a Jack Kerouac novel at two in the morning, when I heard my sixteen-year-old sister sneaking through the front door and beginning the journey to her room. Like a hatched sea turtle heading toward the sea against impossible odds, she serpentined around creaky floorboards and past my parents' room. I was pulling for her, but she stumbled and in a panic sprinted for the stairs. The loudest door in the house opened, and she was busted.

I heard a muffled argument, and I knew my father was pissed that she was drunk.

I raced downstairs as I heard the first slap. I saw red in her cheek, but there were no tears in her eyes. She wouldn't give him that. I never feared anyone the way I feared my father, but that night I didn't even think about it. I stepped between them, planted my feet, and said, "Don't hit a girl. If you want to hit somebody, hit me. You don't hit a girl."

Then I thought, *What the fuck am I doing?*

His face went blank, and I saw that I'd stumped him. I was afraid he was going to hit me, but I put my arm around my sister and led her up the stairs as she started crying. I saw my mother sitting on her bed and my brother peering out his door, still shocked that I wasn't dead. Five minutes later, I was strangely calm as my dad came into my room. He told me to stand up. I knew what was coming . . . but it didn't. Instead he played his trump card.

"You ever cross me again in my house, you're out. No college, nothing. You got that?"

"Yes. I got it."

Standing up to my father came only after I'd left the house and begun feeling better about myself. This act, which years before would have been unthinkable because of my fear of my father, would have been just as unthinkable because it challenged what was acceptable in my family. To stand up to your father is to grow past him, and that is every father's worst fear. Obsolescence: outliving your youthfulness within the family you have created. The entire family is wired to protect the family order and upsetting it is the definition of revolution. I did not revel in it. That night he glared at me, but instead of fear I felt something different—almost like pity. I'd like to say that from that night forward, my life changed and I never feared or needed to test authority again. But life doesn't work like that.

That was the last summer vacation I spent back at home. The following summer, I rented a house in Newport, Rhode Island, with twenty-one other degenerates.

The house was actually a converted barn, which became more and more appropriate as the summer went on.

I was excited by a project I undertook with my brother. We started a business in Newport called Shore Thing Home Services. We advertised that we were a full-service operation: landscaping, housecleaning, catering, transportation, and so forth. We put ties on and visited Realtors' offices, convincing them we had some clue about what we were doing. My brother used his

Me and my brother in Newport. We look so happy here. We must be about to punch some guy in the face.

Me in Newport. I'm not giving the finger; my hand was naturally stuck in this position until I turned thirty.

legendary charm and within a week we had more projects lined up than we could ever handle. The business plan was to charge $15 an hour and pay our friends $10 an hour to actually do the work. On paper, it was an outstanding plan. In reality, our friends were alcoholics and we had no managerial skill whatsoever.

By the end of the summer, three different people were suing us. Mr. Leicherman had hired us to open the pool at his condominiums complex. By July, his tenants staged a rent strike over the algae on the surface of their pool. A driveway-sealing job for another client washed away during a rain shower the day after we did it. Thousands of dollars' worth of Japanese plants in another client's garden were killed. A couple running a bed-and-breakfast hired us to maintain a twelve-foot hedge that ran the perimeter of their one-acre property. Armed with only a nine-inch pair of electric clippers and about seven indoor extension cords, we barely had finished the loop before having to start up again at the beginning.

There can't possibly be a good explanation for this photo, so I'm not going to try.

Drunk girls with low self-esteem. That's how we did it before Internet dating, fellas.

One of the guys in the house was a Tarrytown pal named Chris Reed who is now a state trooper after working the graveyard shift in the South Bronx for five years. Our friend Tommy Bucci visited one weekend but he was not just drinking to have a good time like the other people at the house. The weekend finished badly with Tommy trying to fight a few of us and knocking furniture over. I could see that things were getting bad for Tommy. I spent the next couple of years trying to help him get to AA meetings and find some direction in his life. Back then it was not a good sign if I was the one trying to help you with your drinking.

One Friday night, my brother, a friend, and I were walking home from seeing a band, when some local Rhode Island kids harassed us. I started swinging, and five minutes later I was in jail until Monday morning when the judge came in. The funny thing is that the kid I was fighting was white. The kid in the jail cell next to me was black. And by "funny," I mean that the police sometimes arrest black people for no reason.

We left Newport late one night in our Plymouth Volare station wagon. While Shore Thing Home Services proved to be a failure, it taught me that working for myself was without a doubt how I would be making my living. There was no way anyone else would hire me.

Laughing My Way in
the General Direction of the Bank

A dirty joke is a sort of mental rebellion.

—George Orwell

YAHOO! Graduates of BU's College of Liberal Arts celebrate after ceremonies.   Staff photo by Ted Fitzgerald

Yay! Now we're a bunch of unemployed alcoholics!

Pulling into Boston for my senior year, the procession of U-Hauls with Jersey plates and kids with toaster ovens under their arms lacked the excitement it held for me three years prior. Deirdre had joined me at Boston University as a freshman. She immediately became part of my group of friends at school, and this ended up being one of the most fun years of my life.

With eight months until graduation, I still had no idea what I wanted to do. But as I slowed past Stitches Comedy Club on Boylston Street, I knew this was something I needed to give a real shot. The first step on the road to becoming a paid comedian in 1989 in Boston was Stitches on Sunday nights. I started signing up for Sunday night "Comedy Hell," where, as host George McDonald said week after week, "Welcome to Comedy Hell, where the pipe dreams of a handful of chuckleheads can soar as high as the lights on Broadway or crash and burn in that fiery pit known only as Comedy Hell.

"Comedy Hell! Where the jokes never work, the crowd never laughs, and the show never ends! P.S. We're out of alcohol."

Sign-ups happened in the late afternoon, and then you returned to the club before showtime to see whether or not your name had made the list. If my name did make the list, my heart raced, and I felt one step closer to becoming a comedian. The other comics were from all different walks of life, but the consistent traits among the ones who made it were a fierce competitiveness and a hunger for stage time.

I still have the calendars from my early years in Boston, and there was rarely a night I was not doing a set somewhere. I would hop into a car with Joe Rogan or any of the dozens of hungry up-and-coming comics at the time and drive; one night in Providence, the next in Worcester, the next in Cape Cod. At first we did it for free; we were so desperate for stage time that we would stack chairs or seat people before the show in exchange for an unpaid five minute spot in front of twenty drunks. It was the greatest feeling in the world. I would tape every set and listen to it the next day looking for trims, tags, or segues. Mostly we were getting our stage legs. It was comedy boot camp structured to make you fail. The club owners knew how hard it was to handle Boston audiences so they thinned out the herd and toughened up the ones with potential.

Most clubs had one of the best acts in town host the show. These veterans would go up and destroy the crowd until they could barely breathe. The host would then introduce a shivering nobody who had five minutes to prove that he shouldn't kill himself in the alley behind the club after his set. It was saloon comedy, and you had twenty seconds to gain control of the room before a humiliating silence smothered the place, broken only by verbal darts delivered in thick, hateful Boston "English."

One of the most hurtful things ever said while I was onstage was actually unintentional. A middle-aged couple sat politely in the front row, and during an ego rape of utter quiet after a punch line, I overheard the woman whisper to the man, "the poowa bastahd . . ."

The acts who continually did this began earning small amounts of money for doing twenty minutes in a "club" that was often the back room of a pizza place or the banquet room in a Chinese restaurant. More important, however, was picking up and driving home the headliners, most of whom had lost their licenses after serial DWIs.

I'd never wanted anything in my life the way I wanted to be a good comedian. Fame or even a career (a word that was literally never used in those days) was not part of the equation. I felt honored to be doing this and only wanted more stage time so I could be better. The people in a position to bestow this on me were, for the most part, comedy lovers, and each booked shows in their own way. Out of town headliners with big TV credits rarely survived the "who the fuck are you" greeting from the Boston audiences. And since only about six local comedians had the name value to draw a crowd, the criterion for work was just ability (this is very rare in show business). Oh yeah, and the presumptive burying of your face in the ass of the booker.

Fellow comic and extreme social deviant Tom Cotter would drive out to Newton on Friday afternoons with a case of Sam Adams and aggressively hit on several overworked and under-hit-on college bookers. We generally left with a couple of well-paying college gigs in our Day Runners.

Another phenomenal gig was at a place called The Comedy Vault. It was a converted bank where comedians sold tickets, cleared tables, and did stand-up for no money. The fact that it used to be a bank only makes me laugh now.

Throughout college, just walking past Stitches on my way to class made me nervous because I wanted to be in there so badly. I had performed there once and had done a few college comedy nights on campus, but it was all I thought about. Now I was putting my name down on a list right after Tony "The Machine" Tortoni, who I believe may have done some time for rolling back odometers at his day job as a used car salesman. Another act, A Couple of Broads, was a female duo. One of them wound up an executive producer on *MADtv* for twelve years; the other went into late-night spank TV. It was must-see TV for every comic in New England

I'm not really proud of the jokes I did at first, but the feeling of euphoria was the same as it had been in high school. I never looked back. I spent the next year in class every day and in the comedy clubs most nights. By the time I graduated, I was getting paid gigs.

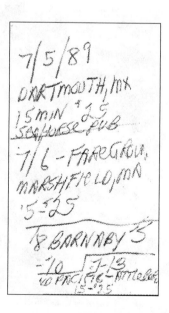

This is my first contract. Written on the back of Jonathon McGuire's business card are the dates and what I would be paid. Thanks, Jonathon.

My first paycheck.

Boston, at this time, had a lot of gigs but twice as many comics who wanted them. Still, a year out of college, and I was making about $500 per week in cash as an opening act. I said what I wanted, wore what I wanted, and the booze was free.

And the fans!

During the day, I played softball with a group of then-struggling comics

Normally, the only guys women like this notice are bodybuilders on steroids. Thank you, comedy!

132

like Dave Cross, Sarah Silverman, Louis C.K. and a lot of other amazingly talented people.

It was in Boston that I was lucky enough on two occasions to see a guy from Texas come to town. Bill Hicks commanded the stage with a conviction greater than anybody I've ever seen. He humiliated average thinking. He would rail against religion, mediocrity, and anybody who failed to agree with him. But he did it with an eloquence and originality that converted more often than offended. More importantly, he was genuinely mad up there. He was expressing deep raw shit as if he needed to get it out or it would kill him. This was the kind of comedy that I wanted to do. It was truthful insofar as Bill Hicks believed everything he was saying in his material. I saw him walk most of the crowd one night because they were not coming along on his ride. He clearly enjoyed it.

When I was onstage, I was experimenting with "Who is the authority in this room right now?" Was it the audience, with its numbers and judgment? They're all looking at me and listening without interrupting. They've invested in me a trust that I am going to make them laugh. Ultimately, the audience will decide if they laugh or not. They've got all the power. But if they are captivated, and laughing and wanting more, then who has the power? *They* need *me*.

Hecklers, most comics' worst nightmare, quickly became my favorite part of performing. Hecklers are the jocks and other assorted douche bags who had intimidated me through my early life. But now, with a microphone and a spotlight on me, they didn't stand a chance, and I went out of my way to annihilate them. One particular night, however, it went badly. I'd been working for about a year when I had a fistfight with a heckler right onstage. His name was Simcha, and I remember because I told him that that was the name of the village idiot in Woody Allen's *Love and Death*. He was a taxi driver who'd just gotten out of the Israeli army.

It was Jewish Singles Comedy Night at Stitches (which I needed several of after the fight). Simcha wanted to meet a woman, but the Jewish women there were rich Boston University girls who were not interested in a real Jew—and definitely not if he drove a taxi for a living. They wanted rich Jewish boys from Long Island. He was already in a bad mood.

It started with Simcha adding his own punch lines to my act. I gently broke down his life for him in front of a laughing crowd. He drew a line in the sand: "You will say nothing more!" I immediately said, "Nothing more." He charged the stage with fists clenched. *My* stage. The stage on which I had earned my place and that I would defend the way he had defended the Gaza Strip or his right to sell electronics at insane prices on Forty-seventh Street in Manhattan.

I cracked him across the top of his head with the microphone before he got me in a headlock and whipped me around the stage like a rag doll. My legs spun around, and I took out the front tables with them. When the bouncers finally finished smoking their joint out back, they came in and dragged Simcha out. The front tables were set back up again, and the club manager, Harry Conforte, told me I had five minutes left in my set. I thought he was kidding, but the host reintroduced me as I stumbled back onstage with a stiff neck to receive my very first standing ovation. I saw Harry smiling in the back of the room. He realized already what I had just learned: in Boston, they'd rather see a fistfight than a comedy show any night of the week. He booked me back for the following weekend.

My calendar started filling up. The best jobs were "corporate gigs." These were well-paying and hard to come by, and they required professionalism and good taste by the comedian. And yet I would still get hired to do them occasionally.

A big advertising agency in Boston once hired me and fellow comedian Joe Rogan to perform at the New England Aquarium, which it had rented out for its annual "Blow Themselves for Promoting Crap to the Public" meeting. The clever twist that only an overpaid advertising "creative" type could think of was that they did not want stand-up, they just wanted us to roam among the crowd and "be funny." It was the most awkward experience of my life until I started eating off people's plates, and Rogan somehow got on the sound system and announced that a boy in a plaid shirt was floating in the shark tank. We were asked to leave.

At another private event, I was asked not to make jokes about "assholes, colons, or rectums." After bombing for about seven minutes, I busted out every asshole joke I could think of. Suddenly the crowd loved me. Except

I also am responsible for ruining what had been a really nice gig at a beautiful four-star hotel up in New Hampshire.

April 9, 1993

Dear Larry,

As you know The Balsams Hotel is one of the most respected and established resorts in the country. When we were first approached by your company about using standup comedians as part of our entertainment, we were apprehensive, to say the least. Last night Greg Fitzsimmons reminded us why.

I greeted Greg before the show and told him to enjoy the show but please refrain from using the "F" word during his performance. Greg then took the stage and began his show by explaining to the crowd that the owner had told him not to use the word "FUCK". When he was finished his act he was told by the maitre'D to pack his bags and leave the premises immediately.

I would hope that in the future, any performers sent to the Balsams by your company would be instructed on the proper etiquette for performing in a five star hotel. If not, I'm afraid that we will cease to use your company's services.

Sincerely,

Howard Rosen
Entertainment Director

My bad. I thought you said, "Say 'fuck' constantly . . ."

for the people running the event. I was not paid for that particular engagement.

Part of me felt ashamed when these things occurred, but the shame was quickly replaced by an asinine pride that I had dared to "fight back." I learned over time that if you take a gig, you have to play by the rules, or don't take the job. The money you are paid as a stand-up is often inversely proportional to the degree you must "play by their rules."

Private shows for corporate parties usually mean not cursing or talking about sex. They are often in vapid banquet rooms with bad sound and a team of waiters serving cheesecake while you are on stage. And the money is phenomenal.

My mentor in comedy, and one of my best friends, is comedian Kevin Meaney. No one has ever made me cry with laughter as hard as Kevin. But we have different styles of comedy. He told me early on that you should do an act that you could show your mother. Of all the things he told me over the years, this rule didn't seem right to me.

It was at this time that I would enter into the annals of Boston comedy lore for humiliating a very shady booking agent named Billy Brown. Young comics still tell me they've heard this story. Billy, despite making a fortune over the years booking shitty comedy rooms all over New England, now owed money to every comic in Boston. On Monday mornings, his bank had four or five comedians all trying to cash bad checks. It got to the point where Billy started paying off his debts to comics for fifty cents on the dollar. I nicknamed him "Potter," after the unscrupulous banker from *It's a Wonderful Life*.

Billy worked with a woman named Carla, who was the toughest woman I'd ever met. One weekend, I worked for her up in Maine. That same weekend, one of her kids was locked up for stealing hubcaps off a police car. She was waiting on Sunday for me to drop off the check from the club. Instead I made the club owner cash it, and I kept it as a down payment on the money that she and Billy owed me. I got the rest of the money about a month later.

I worked for Billy at a degrading comedy room in the back of the Peking Garden restaurant in Shrewsbury, Massachusetts. Before I went onstage, I asked Billy if I could borrow his gold watch because I had forgotten mine and didn't want to go long. After the show, I ducked out the back door. The next morning, he called looking for his watch. Having already had it appraised for $3,000, he met me at a Dunkin' Donuts with an envelope containing the $1,200 that he owed me.

I used to call my dad with these stories, and he would laugh his ass off. He was living vicariously through my adventures in the clubs. When I saw his friends, they always asked me about the stories. I continued sending him letters that were far more intimate than what I could ever say to him face to face.

By the end of 1990, I was cruising along in my newfound career as a carefree drunken joke. With a total workweek of about four to five hours, it all seemed a little too easy. On December 4 I took part in a proud tradition that combined the charitable nature of South Bostonians with their thirst for prostitution and strippers. The show was called "Tits for Tots," and it was held in the red-light district at Nick's Comedy Stop. Comedians performed onstage while strippers and hookers walked around topless collecting money for the Children's Hospital. Just picture the joy on a sick kid's face knowing that each drip into his IV was financed by some union guy from Southie groping a hooker and laughing at dick jokes.

I sat and watched the show, drinking pitchers with some guys I played hockey with from West Roxbury. When I got up onstage, I suddenly felt disoriented. I was drunk. I could not remember my jokes. I just stood there feeling sick. I felt small again. None of the power that I had become accustomed to experiencing onstage was there. When I returned to the table where my teammates sat, things became awkward, and I left. The next day was a real low point in my life. I had been drinking a lot ever since I was about thirteen, and it seemed to always end the same way.

I got to a point where drinking was no longer rebellious. When I started drinking as a teenager, I wasn't allowed to drink. It was illegal, so I had to sneak around. That is when drinking is cool. You have to get a fake ID, find a place to buy it, find somewhere else to drink it, and then sneak in somewhere drunk. If you get away with it, you're lying in bed drunk, your heart is pounding, you've got vomit on your chin, and you're like, "I'm a rebel!"

But that day, I knew the revolution was over. Friends I grew up with were still sitting in Cha Cha's—the same bar, on the same stool, listening to the same Lynyrd Skynyrd songs while doing shots of Jack Daniel's and screaming "I'm a rebel!" No, you're not. You're an alcoholic. What are you rebelling against now? A job? A home to call your own?

That was the last time I drank alcohol, and I wish I could say that my life has changed with my newfound clarity. But life just doesn't work that way.

I had been to many Adult Child of Alcoholics meetings in the previous year because of what I'd been going through with my father, but Alcoholics Anonymous meetings didn't do anything for me. I became, and still am, what is known as a "white knuckle" alcoholic. It comes from my pride in being self-reliant to a fault. I had difficulty going to AA or therapy or even just asking a friend for help. The Irish culture sees accepting help of any kind as being weak. We prefer handling things the old-fashioned way: poorly, and at the expense of others around us.

Meanwhile, I felt almost like I was betraying my family and friends by quitting. There was a lot of resentment from the guys I was living with at the time. "Fitzy, you don't need to quit! You drink less than any of us." At the time, five of us lived in an apartment with no food or toilet paper but a tapped keg seven days a week. I moved out.

Back home, I began to feel like the black sheep for having actually stopped drinking. At a restaurant one night, I told my father that I was feeling stressed out. His solution? Have a drink.

"Everyone needs to get a buzz on once in a while to relax."

"Thanks, Dad."

He really hated that I quit. And I hated feeling like I could do something that he could not. The longer I stayed sober, the more I'd get angry about this. He should have done it for us and he should have done it for himself. I know now that he had different issues than I do, but then I also know what a difference it could have made.

One of my first shows after quitting was, unfortunately, at the Aku-Aku Restaurant in Worcester, Massachusetts. The booze was not in glasses but in giant wooden bowls. I hit the stage following a guy in a clam costume who sang Muddy Waters's "I'm a Man," but as "I'm a Clam." Get it? The crowd obviously loved it. A woman was passed out in the front row. Two gentlemen at her table took turns grabbing her left tit. Now it was my turn to entertain them. I opened with a joke about a Deadbeat Father's Day card. A guy in the middle of the crowd stood up and screamed, "Hey, I'm a deadbeat dad, and I resent that joke!" From three rows back, a biker yelled, "Sit down, asshole!"

The ensuing fistfight simply would not end. Fifteen to twenty guys beat the shit out of one another for so long that the cops got there while the fight was still going on. I announced a play-by-play of the brawl right through to when the cops finally led the last bloody drunk out the door. The comatose fondling victim then awoke and immediately projectile vomited all over the front of the stage and my shoes. I somehow managed to do my closing bit and get out of there. I may have lost a good pair of shoes, but I felt powerful. I was funnier than them, and I wasn't drunk.

While still living in Boston, I spent a summer in an acting program at the prestigious Neighborhood Playhouse School of the Theatre in New York City—although I was almost thrown out halfway through due to an incident in my dance class.

The part of me that knew I was not gay was still slightly threatened by having to participate in a daily dance class. I dealt with it the same way I had dealt with writing papers in high school. I went conceptual and funny. We were required to choreograph and perform a dance, and I chose the theme song from *Fame*. I slopped together some crude break-dancing moves and a backflip before heading out the studio door, down three flights of stairs, and onto West Fifty-fourth Street. A fellow student held a boom box out the windows as I, à la the movie, danced with strangers on the street and at one point rolled over the hood of a taxicab. The class went wild as I returned to the studio for a final backspin. However, the head of the school was very upset when he found out what had happened and put me on probation for the rest of the summer. But it ended up being an amazing experience, and I was invited to join the two-year program, which I did a year later.

I spent part of the summer at my dad's apartment. On some mornings, my dad would promote me on his radio show, and he would come out to see me do stand-up, always beaming with pride. He knew he was responsible for me being up there. There is no other career I could have gone into that would have made my father more proud. I talk to some comics who had to deal with resistance from their families. I had to ask mine to please come to fewer shows.

But I also spent a few nights taking my father home from bars. His brother, Jimmy, the only remaining member of his family, had just died, and it was a difficult time for my dad. The wake was the most surreal mix of people I'd ever seen in my life. Jimmy's pals from his hotel in the Bowery paid their respects alongside my father's country club friends. Most had grown up in the same neighborhood, and it's arguable which group would have won in a drinking contest. That previous summer had brought up a lot of resentment for me. I had been exposed to Al-Anon meetings and had quit drinking myself. (I actually never drank *myself*, but I saw a guy in a porno do it once, and it seemed wrong.)

I was very uncomfortable watching my father destroy himself and treat his family poorly. To add to all the turmoil, a few months earlier, he had been let go from his radio show on WNEW, where he'd worked on and off for twenty-five years. He'd just had a great run for a couple of years doing a show with the very talented Al Rosenberg. Al's smothering, close relationship with his wife and kids ran headlong into my dad's accounts of partying his way around Manhattan. The result was very funny and it seemed like the show would go on for a long time.

When it didn't, I sent him a letter to try cheering him up.

Again, the letter was never acknowledged. I don't know how I had become so sensitive and nurturing, but I knew that, at the very least, it made my father uncomfortable. I began to wonder if my father might even think that my sending him these letters meant I was gay. Those were my two major fears in life: that a stranger would punch me in the face and that my father would be convinced I was gay.

I returned home from Boston in the fall to do a show in Princeton, New Jersey. My folks headed down to attend the show and spend the night. Following the show, my dad callously critiqued my stand-up, saying I needed to write more. This hurt a lot to hear. Having just seen him in pretty poor shape all summer, who was he to now criticize my work?

I was confused about a lot of things and found it hard to be around my parents, so for the first time in my life, I decided to take some very painful

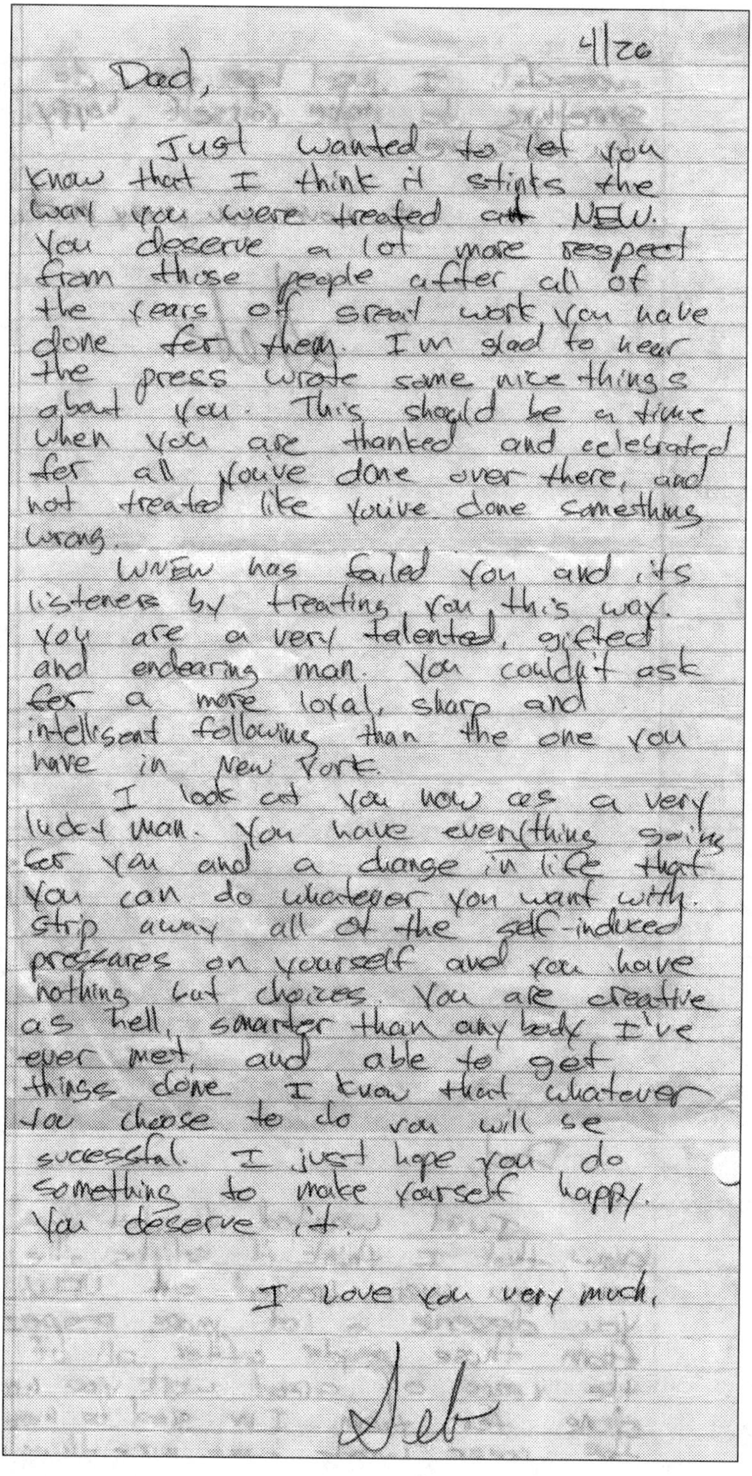

4/26

Dad,

Just wanted to let you know that I think it stinks the way you were treated at NEW. You deserve a lot more respect from those people after all of the years of great work you have done for them. I'm glad to hear the press wrote some nice things about you. This should be a time when you are thanked and celebrated for all you've done over there, and not treated like you've done something wrong.

WNEW has failed you and its listeners by treating you this way. You are a very talented, gifted and endearing man. You couldn't ask for a more loyal, sharp and intelligent following than the one you have in New York.

I look at you now as a very lucky man. You have everything going for you and a change in life that you can do whatever you want with. Strip away all of the self-induced pressures on yourself and you have nothing but choices. You are creative as hell, smarter than anybody I've ever met, and able to get things done. I know that whatever you choose to do you will be successful. I just hope you do something to make yourself happy. You deserve it.

I love you very much,

Jeb

```
              April 1, 1993

Dear Greg,

I haven't been ready to write to you.  I wanted to
deal with our situation before I made comment.
Your letter was very touching, and made me realize
how upset your life has been.  I hate having you
sad, but your struggle should make you strong.
██████████████████████████████████████████████████
██████████████████████████████████████████████████
████████████████████████ During this period of time, it
would have been almost impossible for me to
communicate with them and still move forward.
There is no question your decision to break away
hurt me very much.  There are times I don't
understand and would like to call you and yell -
stop, enough.  But you have your own time table.
I felt so close to you, as a son and a friend.
Sharing as we did, is something I'm only
comfortable doing with a very few people.

You had invited us for Thanksgiving but never
followed up.  That's when I knew you were cutting
me off.
```

time apart from them. I was trying to keep from drinking while going to therapy to deal with the depression and anger I had felt my entire life. When I didn't come home for Thanksgiving and Christmas that year, my father stopped talking to me. He could not understand what he felt to be a total rejection.

I received this letter from my mother about six months after my gig in Princeton.

This seeming betrayal was compounded by the fact that my father and my brother, who had always had a difficult relationship, were not speaking. Deirdre had been steadily migrating west for about three years, finally settling in Alaska. They were not communicating very often. We were all struggling with creating our own lives out from under my father's judgmental and powerful presence. The irony was that he had actually stopped drinking that fall for what turned out to be the rest of his life. Meanwhile, I was putting up boundaries and standing up for myself, because I believed that the cycle of his drinking and attempts to control me would continue if I didn't.

As much as he was hurt by my actions, and although my intention was not to change him, my pulling away may have had something to do with him finally quitting.

During this period that I was out of touch, my father came across a young couple begging in the street. Rather than just give them some change or leftovers, he invited them to move into his apartment. Knowing all along that they were drug addicts and could not be trusted, my father still gave them a chance. My mother told me that he said that they reminded him of his own kids, and it broke his heart to see them out on the street. He came home from work one day to find his apartment cleaned out. Apparently he was not angry. He knew that he had given them a chance, and that for the rest of their lives, these two people would have to live with the fact that they had, unfortunately, done exactly what was expected of them.

The Sad Part Where Dad Dies

Do not go gentle into that good night. Rage, rage against the dying of the light.

—Dylan Thomas

(NY Times)

June 4, 1993
Bob Fitzsimmons, Personality on TV And the Radio, 53

By GLENN COLLINS

Bob Fitzsi mmons, a New York radio and television host known fo r his wry intervi ews with celebrity guests, died on Wed nesday. He was 53 and lived in Ta rrytow n, N.Y.

He collapsed at a M anhattan restaurant and was taken to Metropolitan Hospital, where he was pronounce d dead, said his son Bob.

Mr. Fitzsi mmons was noted for his silky - voiced radio anecdotes during the "morning - drive" ti me period at WNEW -AM, wh ere he was host with a partne r, Al Rosenber g, from 1989 to 1991. He had his own sho w from 1991 until the station changed its fo rmat to all - business progra mming late last year, becoming WBBR.

He was also a host of the "Jerry Le wis Muscula r Dystrophy Telethon " from 1973 until 1989, and was one of the original hosts of the Channe l 5 morning television sho w, "Good Day New York."

Born Aug. 14, 1939 in Queens, M r. Fitzsimmons g rew up in the Riverdal e section of the Bronx and was a graduate of All - Hallows High School in the Bron x and Boston University.

In 1962 Mr. Fitzsi mmons bega n his broadcasting c areer at WNEW as an assistant to Te d Brown and William B. Williams. He also appea red as the char acter Trevo r Traffic with the radio team of Gene Kla van and Bob Finch. A fter becoming a radio host and disk jockey at WRKL in Rocklan d County, N.Y., he mo ved to WFMJ in Youngstow n, Ohio, and then to WPEN in Philadelphia.

Mr. Fitzsi mmons returned to New York in 1970 to beco me a talk-show host for radio station WHN, and then returned to WNEW - AM fro m 1973 to 1979 as host of the "aft ernoon driv e" prog ramming slot. Subsequently he was a talk-sho w host and announcer for WAB C radio before returning to WNEW -AM.

In addition to his son Bob, of New Y ork City, he is survived by his wife, Patric ia; anothe r son, Gre g of Boston, and a daughter, Deird re, of Ska gw ay, Alaska.

Bob Fitzsimmons dead at 53; veteran radio broadcaster

By ALICE McQUILLAN
Daily News Staff Writer

Bob Fitzsimmons, 53, the veteran radio broadcaster whose wit and humor sustained a 30-year career, died Wednesday of a heart attack he suffered while dining in upper Manhattan.

Known as "Fitz" to viewers, listeners and friends, the long-time talk show host was best known for his work on WNEW-AM, which was sold last year.

Starting as a gofer there in 1962, he was host of various programs, most recently a popular morning show — first with Al Rosenberg and then by himself.

In television, Fitzsimmons was an early co-anchor of Channel 5's "Good Day New York" and the long-time New York co-host of Jerry Lewis' Labor Day telethon. He was also a staff announcer for WABC radio and a host of programs on the ABC radio network, on the former WHN in New York and at radio and TV stations in Youngstown, Ohio.

His was the voice on many television and radio commercials.

'Never let truth get in the way'

"He was funny, a great humorist and raconteur who never let the truth get in the way of telling a funny story," said Don Buchwald, his friend and agent.

Active in the Friars Club, Fitzsimmons became the group's scribe and often was the host of charity benefits.

Born in Bayside, Queens, he was reared in the Riverdale section of the Bronx and attended All Hallows High School and then Boston University.

He is survived by his wife, Patricia, two sons, Robert and Gregory, and a daughter, Deirdre.

The wake will be at the Dwyer Funeral Home in Tarrytown, N.Y., from 2 p.m. to 4 p.m. and from 7 p.m. to 9 p.m. tomorrow and Sunday.

A funeral Mass will be offered at 11 a.m. Monday at the Church of the Transfiguration in Tarrytown.

Bob Fitzsimmons
Radio personality

Bob Fitzsimmons, a veteran New York radio and television host known for his interviews with celebrities suffered a heart attack at a restaurant and died Wednesday. He was 53.

Fitzsimmons was best known for his work on WNEW-AM in New York, where he began as a clerk in 1962. He worked as a Deejay at WRKL in Pomona from 1984 to 1985.

After becoming a radio host at WRKL in Rockland County, he moved to WFMJ in Youngstown, Ohio, and WPEN in Philadelphia before returning to New York in 1970. He returned to WNEW in 1973.

Fitzsimmons was one of the original hosts of WNYW-TV's "Good Day New York." He was also a host of the "Jerry Lewis Muscular Dystrophy Telethon" from 1973 to 1989.

At WRKL, Fitzsimmons began a contest called "Hotsy Totsy," where he would play obscure songs and callers could phone in and win prizes. Friend and onetime coworker, WRKL Deejay and Music Director Steve Possell said Fitzsimmons was a pioneer in talk radio.

While at WRKL, Fitzsimmons began a program called "Feminine Forum," where women could call in and talk about their problems. "He had an incredible way of drawing information from people who called in," Possell said.

"Bob was extremely outgoing and amiable," Possell said, "he had an incredible one-on-one relationship with the listener."

Fitzsimmons is survived by his wife, Patricia Fitzsimmons of Tarrytown; two sons, Robert Fitzsimmons of Manhattan and Gregory Fitzsimmons of Boston; and a daughter, Deirdre Fitzsimmons of Skagway, Alaska.

A service will be held 11 a.m., Monday, June 7 at the Church of the Transfiguration, South Broadway, Tarrytown. Calling hours are today and tomorrow from 2 to 4 and 7 to 9 p.m. at the Dwyer Funeral Home, 90 N. Broadway, Tarrytown.

Remembering 'Fitz'

The death of Bob Fitzsimmons, 53, from an apparent heart attack on June 2 should not go unnoticed by those who love radio and New York. "Fitz," as he was known by friends and listeners alike, was a quick-witted and thoroughly affable broadcaster who worked in a long list of forums.

He disc-jockeyed on the now-defunct WNEW-AM, did network talk shows on ABC Talkradio, co-hosted the annual Jerry Lewis telethon, inaugurated WNYW-TV's "Good Day New York" and returned to WNEW-AM for a three-year run of morning duty that ended in 1992. He was an active member of the Friars Club and a man with a million friends.

It was on wake-up duty on WNEW-AM that Fitz displayed some of his best licks, as a co-host with comedian Al Rosenberg and as a verbal sparring partner with former Mayor Ed Koch, who discussed the news on the program (and sometimes met his match in the feisty Irishman). Though Fitz and Al's was an entertainment show, complete with put-on voices and bits, Fitz made it clear off the air that he hoped their Irish-Jewish humor helped break down barriers in the polyglot city. And it did.

"Bob was good fun; he had a good sense of humor," Koch recalled. "I can remember I once had him and his wife over to my apartment for dinner, and he brought me a house-warming gift, an Irish teacup, which I use every morning. And he taught me the trade! Back then, I was just Ed Koch. Now [on WABC], I'm the Voice of Reason."

Fitz: a star that shined for all

DICK RYAN

'Fitz was a celebrity the day he was born.'

I am more than a little irritated by the Daily News.

Last week, in a fit of sheer snobbery, the News printed a half-page diagram of Madison Square Garden, pinpointing the exact sections and seats where Woody Allen, Connie Chung and their super-celebrity ilk would be sitting for The Big Knicks Game.

However — and this is a large however — they failed to print a similar diagram of the Barrister Coffee Shop in Brooklyn Heights, where the day generally begins for me and where a good cup of coffee is a hell of a lot more crucial than a Ewing slam-dunk.

But there wasn't a single diagram of the Barrister.

Without a diagram of the Barrister, there was not a trace of Mike from the city job in his usual seat at the counter, or of Anna the waitress pouring that great second cup, or of L'arold the attorney sitting in his usual end booth reading the paper, or Terry the secretary waiting for her change by the back register.

About a week ago, a friend of mine died who was very much a celebrity and every inch the kind of guy who could slide onto one of the counter stools at the Barrister, strike up a conversation with Mike and Anna, and casually ask Jack the owner for the breakfast special.

Bob Fitzsimmons, radio and television star, dead of a heart attack at 53, had this one great weakness that I always knew about and that I exploited without the slightest shame.

In all the years when I've been involved in three separate Brooklyn charities simply because I got paid for it, all I had to do was pick up the phone and Fitz would be there as roastmaster, master of ceremonies, guest celebrity.

Without hesitation. Without a nickel in return. And always with that great kidding laugh. His arm

around the shoulder of the whole room, he would walk around, stopping here and there, just one of the boys like a guy from the Barrister, making everybody feel as if they were the celebrity.

The last time I was with him, he had come out again to a fundraiser we were having for infants with AIDS.

Like always, he just faded into the crowd and hung around and then disappeared near the end without a word, without any of the celebrity noise and nonsense. He would be getting up at four that morning for his radio show, but it didn't matter. It never did.

"How did you get involved in this kind of thing, Ryan?" he laughed as we walked to the door. "These are all nice people."

Fitz was a celebrity the day he was born and it had nothing to do with pizzazz and showtime. He celebrated humor and the people around him and even the people he would never meet. He celebrated family and friends and the good things that he quietly did for others.

Fitz was always supremely Fitz and, in that, he was warmer, more genuine and far more human than any dot on a newspaper diagram. He was, from beginning to end, one of us.

So long, Fitz. See you next time. And hey, thanks for coming by.

Dick Ryan is a free-lance contributor who appears regularly.

BOB FITZSIMMONS

1939 ~ 1993

Friar Bob Fitzsimmons passed away on June 2, 1993

We dedicate this issue of the *Friars Epistle* in loving memory to our beloved Scribe and valued member of the Board of Governors for his unfailing dedication and loyalty to the Club and to this newspaper. Fitz's presence, his voice and his writings will be missed. We have been truly fortunate that he has passed through our Monastery doors and into our hearts.

The Board of Governors has decided to rename the annual golf outing in memory of Bob Fitzsimmons, "The Friars Annual Bob Fitzsimmons Golf and Tennis Tournament."

JACK L. GREEN
JACK L. GREEN
Dean

THE NEW YORK TIMES OBITUARIES FRIDAY, JUNE 4, 1993

Bob Fitzsimmons, Radio Personality And TV Host, 53

By GLENN COLLINS

Bob Fitzsimmons

Bob Fitzsimmons, a New York radio and television host known for his wry interviews with celebrity guests, died on Wednesday. He was 53 and lived in Tarrytown, N.Y.

He collapsed at a Manhattan restaurant and was taken to Metropolitan Hospital, where he was pronounced dead, said his son Bob.

Mr. Fitzsimmons was noted for his silky-voiced radio sardonics during the "morning-drive" time period at WNEW-AM, where he was host with a partner, Al Rosenberg, from 1989 to 1991. He had his own show from 1991 until the abrupt changes in format to all-business programming late last year, becoming WHN.

He was also a host of the "Jerry Lewis Muscular Dystrophy Telethon" from 1973 until 1989, and was one of the original hosts of the Channel 5 morning television show, "Good Day New York."

Born Aug. 14, 1939 in Queens, Mr. Fitzsimmons grew up in the Riverdale section of the Bronx and was a graduate of All Hallows High School in the Bronx and Iona University.

In 1962 Mr. Fitzsimmons began his broadcasting career at WNEW as an assistant to Ted Brown and William B. Williams. He also appeared as the character Trevor Traffic with the radio team of Gene Klavan and Bob Finch. After becoming a radio host and disk jockey at WNBJ, in Rockland County, N.Y., he moved to WFM1 in Youngstown, Ohio, and then to WPEN in Philadelphia.

Mr. Fitzsimmons returned to New York in 1970 to become a talk-show host for radio station WNN, and then returned to WNEW-AM from 1973 to 1979 as host of the "afternoon drive" programming slot. Subsequently he was a talk-show host and announcer for WABC radio before returning to WNEW-AM.

In addition to his son Bob, of New York City, he is survived by his wife, Patricia; another son, Greg of Skaneateles; and a daughter, Deirdre, of Skagway, Alaska.

Gannett Suburban Newspapers

4B Friday, June 4, 1993

Robert M. Fitzsimmons: radio, TV personality

Robert M. Fitzsimmons, a radio show host from Tarrytown, died Wednesday of a heart attack in Metropolitan Hospital Center in Manhattan. He was 53.

Mr. Fitzsimmons was best-known as a radio personality on WNEW radio's morning show, featuring a format of popular standards. He had worked at WNEW and other New York radio stations for the past 20 years. When WNEW went off the air about six months ago, he became an announcer for Showtime and The Movie Channel on cable television.

"He was a very talented broadcaster and a terrific ad-ent," said his agent, Don Buchwald. "He was also a great raconteur who never let the truth get in the way of a good story."

Mr. Fitzsimmons, a Queens native, was born Aug. 14, 1939, to James L. and Katherine Harrigan Fitzsimmons. After graduating from All Hallows High School in the Bronx, he earned a bachelor of arts degree from Boston University.

On Aug. 10, 1964, Mr. Fitzsimmons married Patricia McCarthy

in County Cavan, Ireland. The couple lived in Tarrytown for the last 22 years.

During the 1970s and 1980s, he served as the New York host for Jerry Lewis' annual Muscular Dystrophy telethon. He also was on the Board of Governors of the Friars Club in New York City.

Mr. Fitzsimmons was on the Board of Directors of the Guardian Angels' home in Brooklyn. He was a member of the Knollwood Country Club. He had been a former coach of Terry-town youth football and baseball teams.

Mr. Fitzsimmons was a parishioner of the Church of the Transfiguration in Tarrytown. He was active in the Knights of Columbus, a Roman Catholic fraternal organization.

Besides his wife, Mr. Fitzsimmons is survived by two sons, Robert Fitzsimmons of Manhattan and Gregory Fitzsimmons of Boston; and a daughter, Deirdre Fitzsimmons of Skagway, Alaska.

A brother, James Fitzsimmons, died July 23, 1992.

Donations in his name are being made to the All Hallows High School Development Fund, 111 E. 164th St., the Bronx, N.Y. 10452.

Arrangements are by the Dwyer Funeral Home in Tarrytown.

NEW YORK POST, FRIDAY, JUNE 4, 1993

RADIO'S BOB FITZSIMMONS DEAD AT 54

Well-known New York radio personality Bob Fitzsimmons collapsed and died of an apparent heart attack at a Manhattan restaurant Wednesday night, friends said yesterday. He was 54.

Fitzsimmons had been a friendly voice on radio since 1970, hosting call-in shows at WABC, WHN and WNEW-AM.

He started his broadcasting career in 1962 as an assistant to WNEW-AM's team of "Klavan and Finch," William B. Williams and Ted Brown.

For many years, co-hosted the Jerry Lewis Labor Day Telethon and had a short stint as co-host of Fox 5's "Good Day, New York."

Fitzsimmons is survived by his wife, Pat, and three children. *Jill Brooke*

RADIO'S BOB FITZSIMMONS DEAD AT 54

Well-known New York radio personality Bob Fitzsimmons collapsed and died of an apparent heart attack at a Manhattan restaurant Wednesday night, friends said yesterday. He was 54.

Fitzsimmons had been a friendly voice on radio since 1970, hosting call-in shows at WABC, WHN and WNEW-AM.

He started his broadcasting career in 1962 as an assistant to WNEW-AM's team of "Klavan and Finch," William B. Williams and Ted Brown.

For many years, co-hosted the Jerry Lewis Labor Day Telethon and had a short stint as co-host of Fox 5's "Good Day, New York."

Fitzsimmons is survived by his wife, Pat, and three children. *Jill Brooke*

6B TIMES ■ SUNDAY, JUNE 6, 1993

justified.

■ ■ ■

BOB FITZSIMMONS, 53, a veteran New York radio and television host, suffered a heart attack at a New York restaurant and died Wednesday. He was best known for his work on WNEW-AM in New York, where he began as a clerk in 1962. He also was one of the original hosts of WNYW-TV's *Good Day New York*, and he was a host of the *Jerry Lewis Muscular Dystrophy Telethon* from 1973 to 1989. ■ ■ ■

'N REMEMBRANCE

Bob Fitzsimmons, who died so suddenly and unexpectedly Wednesday night, was not so much a baseball guy as he was a pal to a lot of baseball guys like Terry Cashman, Rusty Staub and Gene Orza. Fitz was a witty, warm and important radio voice in this town for 30 years. To those who knew him as a pal, he was quite simply a beautiful person. May God bless him.

Bill Madden
Daily News

$\mathbf{T}$wo months after I received my mother's letter, my father died of a heart attack at just fifty-three years of age. It was during the main course while dining in a Harlem restaurant that was frequented by the Mafia. (The clientele, out of habit, quickly exited the establishment.) He had been laughing the moment before with my mother and the young actor from *My Cousin Vinny* (the one who was not Ralph Macchio). He died at a good restaurant, with my mom, having a lot of laughs. He died in the style in which he had lived, and for that I am very grateful.

At the time, though, I can only remember feeling tremendous guilt that I had turned my back on my father at the end of his life. I felt weak that I had to be away to "find myself." Suddenly my sobriety and hours of therapy embarrassed me. He had managed to live his life without any of that; why was I so sensitive that I couldn't do the same?

Going through his finances with my mother, I saw that the man had not only met his responsibilities throughout his life, he even left his house in order in his death. He'd been stockpiling savings for my mother including a large life insurance policy. His last kid had just finished college and his house was almost completely paid for. And then he died.

It was a confusing period for the entire family as we all gathered to bury him and then sort out where we all were and where we were all headed. My mother worked at the Arts & Leisure section of *The New York Times* and brought home movie screeners after the critics had criticized them. The night after the final wake we collapsed on the couch and I rummaged through these videotapes, finally pulling one out that seemed perfect for the situation. It was called, *Daddy's Dyin' . . . , Who's Got the Will?* We laughed so hard we had to pass tissues around the room. The relief from crying happy tears signaled in some small way that we were all going to be alright.

A week after the funeral, I was helping my mom clean out Dad's belongings in his office. I opened the bottom drawer to his desk and found a bundle of letters. Among them were notes that I'd sent to him throughout my entire life. Birthday cards, letters, even postcards. They were in their own pile with a rubber band around them, tucked out of sight as if they were

Aug. 12, '92

DAD,

How are you? You sounded kind of down the other day on the phone, and I know it's hard for you sometimes to talk about how you feel.

You've had a pretty tough summer. Losing Jimmy was probably one of the most difficult things you've ever been through. I'm sure it brings up a lot of different feelings for you about your past and about where you are now. Jimmy was always a strange topic growing up in our family. You always treated Jimmy with respect in front of us and we loved him in a special way, although it was only in the last few years that I started to understand more about him. Through him I learned a lot about you as well. About your fears of being out of control, and your anger at the world. He was your only family for a lot of years. Our family is so important to me that it is hard to imagine that situation. The bond that you two had, as precarious as it was over the years, remained strong until the end. Sometimes I forget how thoughtful and sensitive you are. I will never forget visiting Jimmy in the hospital 6 months ago only to find his room filled with gifts and candy and signs of your concern. As I sat there the phone rang, and it was you checking to see how he was doing.

You need to feel everything you are going through. It is o.k. to be sad or angry or anything else. Our family tries so hard to suppress our feelings and be happy. You will not spiral out of control if you allow yourself some sadness and tears. I hope I don't sound preachy or like I know everything, it's just that I heard your voice and you sounded like you were holding a lot in. It's very hard to feel safe at a time like this and I just want you to know that I'm here if you need me. That's another one of the not-so-bad things I learned from my Dad. How to be caring.

Love Always,

contraband. Looking back, it was the first, but not last, collection of letters that would help me make sense of my life. On top of the pile was the last one I had ever sent him.

I had never stopped talking to my father. I'd been feeling like a piece of shit, thinking that I'd abandoned him prior to his death. But I now saw that I'd reached out to him until the end. My mind raced back to that past Christmas when he refused to get on the phone. My mother told me a week later that my father would not talk to me until I apologized. Realizing that I had not iced him out of my life after all did not make his death any less tragic or painful. It just made it more clear that he had limitations.

DAD

Don't fall from me, my father.
Stay close in my dreams and hold my soul
Close to you and away from the cold.
Keep your strength inside me, guide me, always.

I shake my fist as I stand and wonder
Why you stole from me my last good-bye.
Then my tears turn to laughter and I sigh
As I think about all I stole from you.

I stole your attention, from the day I was born.
I stole your laughter, endless and flowing.
I stole your wisdom, you were the all-knowing.
But my most cherished theft was your love.

It was an easy theft from a wide open vault.
I could see many had been there before.
Broken glass lay unswept on the floor
But the door remained wide and inviting.

I passed often and warmly through that door,
Filling my pockets each time with your treasures.
What you gave to me was love beyond measure,
So I forgive you for stealing my last good-bye.

In a daze on the morning of the funeral, I wrote what many consider to be the worst poem since "I'm Rubber and You're Glue." I read it at the service and there wasn't a wet eye in the house.

Not responding to my letters did not mean that he hadn't been touched by them or that he thought I was a raving homosexual. He simply could not allow himself to go to a place that was unsafe for him. He could provide for his family but he could not allow them in.

My mother describes my dad as very angry during the final nine months of his life, when he'd finally quit drinking. They fought quite a bit, and actually had an argument on the day he died. Luckily, they made up with each other with just hours to spare. If they had not, then he would have passed at a time when he was not on good terms with any member of his family.

In Princeton he'd criticized me, after having always supported my doing comedy. Normally I would have cowered and been ashamed at having not met his expectations. But I was no longer looking for his criticism at this point in my life. It was not his right to critique my stand-up. The same way I protected my stage and my act from Simcha and Billy and Carla and anyone else, I protected it from him. It was my self-worth. My act came out of my family's sense of humor, but it also came from my own refusal to feel weak and powerless in my life. I was not going to let anyone take that away from me.

When Dad passed away, I tracked down Deirdre in Alaska and sent her a ticket to return home. For the previous four years she'd been traveling across the country, heading west, and Alaska is as far as you can go without becoming a Communist. Once she came home for the funeral, she stayed with my mother, spending the next few years by her side making sure she was okay. Today she lives with her own amazing family a few towns over from my mother, and the two remain very close.

Following her lead, I returned to New York as well.

A friend hooked me up with an apartment in Little Italy, right on Mulberry Street. It was a rat-infested tenement six floors above the clubhouse of notorious Mob boss John Gotti: the Ravenite Social Club. Though Gotti had recently been sent to jail, on Wednesday nights the black Lincoln Town Cars still pulled up and deposited the remaining members of the almost defunct Gambino crime family. If you thought the characters in movies like *Goodfellas* and *The Godfather* were played up for the screen, nothing matched the shiny-suited, cannoli-eating tough guys who loitered just below Prince Street in some sacred vigil held for what had been and was no more.

My building was occupied mostly by Italian families that had been there for generations. Their children had long since spilled out to New Jersey or Staten Island, but the older folks had known no other life, nor did they want to. Tony and Gladys Spagnoli were my landlords. Having raised several boys who'd "done well in construction," the Spagnolis now lived around the corner on a ground-floor condo that the boys took care of. The illegal sublet cost the Spagnolis $350 a month, but my end of it was $1,200. Each month, I would stop by their place, where they would make cappuccino as Tony counted out ten one-hundred-dollar bills. When Tony left the room, Gladys would discreetly pocket another $200 from me, saying, "Tony don't need to know about this. It's my bingo money."

St. Patrick's held bingo night on Wednesdays, then on Thursdays the ladies would traipse down to the Shrine Church of Saint Anthony of Padua, on Sullivan Street, for the other bingo night. Tony and the other men frequented the Chinese OTB on Houston Street and slipped dollars to Gina to play the numbers every day. You could give her the money as she almost constantly walked her dog or was at cocktail hour at the Shark Bar on Spring Street.

One of the many perks that came with the apartment was a life insurance policy issued by Tony at least once every time I talked to him: "Anybody bothering you, you tell me. I'll take care of it. I know people. You don't know who I know, but I know people." This was reassuring, as I knew that the Spagnolis had been robbed one Christmas morning and Tony had been stabbed by the fleeing assailant. The story goes that the guys who did it were *taken care of.* That's it.

Everyone in the neighborhood had an angle. The legendary San Gennaro Festival ran right past my place, and I watched in horror as Mayor Rudolph Guiliani's administration gutted it in 1995, claiming that organized crime involvement was in the cash-only fried dough stands and pizza wagons. No shit, Rudy; you're a fucking genius crime stopper. Today the festival exists in name only and resembles every other post-Giuliani event in the city, filled with Peruvian flute bands and handmade necklaces from Chinese factories.

I could tell as I was living there that this was the tail end of a culture that lived within society but by its own rules. Gotti was revered because he bought everyone a turkey at Thanksgiving and made big donations to St. Patrick's Elementary School. Martin Scorsese attended this school, and it is where he shot the opening scenes from *Mean Streets*. Ascending those rickety, slanted stairs of my apartment building each day, I knew that I had several conversations ahead of me, and sometimes excellent leftovers. The doors remained open all day, and the tenants—Carmine, Joe, Vinny, Vinny Girl (both grew up in the building together, so the names were necessary)—each called out, "Hey, Kevin! How ya doin', huh?" For three years, I was called Kevin. I corrected them only for the first two years, then I just let it go.

Another perk that came with the unit was furniture. The tables were a gold veneer with ornate handles. The only thing not worn out on the collapsed sofa was the plastic cover, which matched the plastic cover on the La-Z-Boy chair. Mice could be heard scratching their way across the red tin ceiling, and the always-on radiator hissed out a fishy smell I have thankfully never smelled anywhere since. I remember coming across bullet casings and a phone recording device when I first unpacked. The building sagged so severely that a dropped orange would race across the floor; halfway through a shower, you needed to kick the water toward the drain, or it would overflow the far edge.

I spent more time in this apartment than I should have, only leaving to do comedy and go to acting school. Since I was still not drinking, performing let me escape my pain and deal with it at the same time. I chased down spots at every club in the city, sometimes logging as many as six or seven shows in a night. As my confidence grew onstage, audiences had less and less of an ability to make me question my jokes or even my right to be up there.

Every comedian works toward a state where his energy spent reacting to the crowd's approval is overcome by a belief in himself. I was first introduced to this in Boston, but Bill Hicks epitomized it like nobody else. Now, night after night, I was watching guys like Dave Attell and Dave Chappelle effortlessly take control; the crowd had no say in where they were being taken. When these guys took the stage, a crowd's hostility was suddenly shattered. It was obvious who was in charge.

Authority had always felt crushing—from my father, teachers, and later, my comedy audiences. I was now beginning to redefine this relationship with crowds by simply expressing this resentment. Surviving the sometimes brutal New York City clubs demanded this honesty, but it was also born out of the anger I carried with me and the fact that I suddenly did not care. They could not hurt me the way they could have before and, freed from that, I started to find my own voice.

I was beginning to get my head out of the fog when Jesus Christ orchestrated my next joyful event. My buddy Kyle called to tell me that Tommy Bucci had died. Tommy had gotten into a fight with his girlfriend and was driving in a rage, going the wrong way on a highway. He hit a car head-on and died along with the couple in the other car. It was so hard to believe, yet at the same time, it was not surprising. I'd been very close to Tommy most of my life, and he was one of the kindest, gentlest souls I've ever known. But then he would snap, usually while drinking, and become another person. I could relate to that and yet also was no closer to understanding it than he probably had been.

Tommy belonged inside that stadium. Not only because of his athletic abilities . . . it was already the third quarter, but he wouldn't abandon the keg.

153

Tommy, like me, had tempted fate with his behavior. Where I was able to pull back, however, he and my father were not. My dad died young because he refused to change despite many warnings. Now Tommy was gone because he could not free himself from a path he believed was the only one he was meant to be on. I was haunted by his misfortune and remembered Tommy's reaction to me going to Europe after high school. He told me that he was proud of me and I saw that he had tears in his eyes. I felt then the way I now felt at his funeral: why couldn't he have gone to Europe? Why couldn't he have stopped punishing himself before something like this happened?

Luckily, I was on the road, alone in shitty hotel rooms for weeks at a time to ponder these uplifting questions. The high school prom show I detailed in chapter one might resonate more now that you have read the context of my life during this period. I continued going to therapy, attending twelve-step meetings, and masturbating; anywhere I could find answers. A year later, I knew I could safely abandon all of this touchy-feely "healing" bullshit, because things began heating up in my career. Time to focus on what was really important. Each summer roughly 100 comedians are brought to the amazing city of Montreal for the Just for Laughs comedy festival. The comics perform in front of important people from the entertainment industry in hopes of a development deal for their own TV show. Basically, comedians from New York fly to Canada to convince talent scouts from Los Angeles that they can appeal to middle America (that was a nice fucking sentence). Each year there is one breakout act who very suddenly has a lot of "buzz" and "heat." It spreads like wildfire and everyone *must* have him (or her).

In 1995 that person was me. After I lit up a couple of crowds early in the week, a number of TV executives, casting directors, agents, and managers slipped into the back of a theater one night to watch me.

What resulted was right out of the pages of a poorly written comedian's memoir. As I walked offstage, someone shook my hand and said, "Don't look behind you but a line of executives is forming." I left the theater that night with business cards and promises that actually turned out *not* to be bullshit. Within a month I had a big agent, signed a sitcom development deal with Fox, and most importantly got booked to appear on the *Late Show with David Letterman*.

My calendar started filling up with well-paid headlining gigs and I was able to present my mother with some very nice things that had been written about me.

To this day, the greatest moment I've ever experienced as a comedian was my first appearance on the *Late Show with David Letterman*. My last thought backstage before Biff Henderson patted me on the back and pointed at my mark seventeen steps across that shiny floor was, "Okay, Dad, let's go do this." Six minutes later, having just performed the set of my life, I was behind the curtain again, but now with tears streaming down my face. The following guest, a relative unknown at that time named Faith Hill, saw me and drew me in for a spontaneous good old Southern hug. I don't like country music but I might be in love with Faith Hill.

My family waited for me in the audience and we headed over to Fifty-fifth street for an after-party at a place that meant a lot to us: the Friars Club. I had asked them to put together a simple buffet for fifteen to twenty people. When we arrived, there was a carving station set up, a dessert table, and an open bar. They barely charged me for it. It was a perfect end to the night at a place where my father had spent a large part of his adult life and where we had all felt his presence still.

As the dust settled on what had been an incredible year, the anger that had been driving me was starting to come out in some not-so-productive ways. I reserve judgment on anyone I see who achieves success and starts acting like an asshole. Whatever assholishness lays dormant in you previous to success will spring to life and grow quickly and exponentially. A well-paying gig at Disneyland somehow brought out my angry side.

The following year I hosted a game show on MTV called *Idiot Savants*. It was an intense production schedule. We'd shoot four episodes a day, five days a week. The ratings were not bad, and the reviews were pretty good. I was not very appreciative of my good fortune, however, and, looking back, I behaved kind of like a douche. I did an interview with *Time Out New York* magazine that did not help us get renewed for the following season.

Another opportunity which I managed to take a giant shit on was right around the corner. A buddy of mine named Ross Brockley (a farmer from Nebraska, and, yes, that is his real name) and I had started shooting a

My first appearance on
Letterman. To this day,
the single best moment in
my professional life.

When you take a job
at Disneyland, leave
the attitude back at
the tram. My lawyer
had to fight to get me
paid on this one.

Re: Greg Fitzsimmons

Dear Mr. Botelho:

We are the attorneys for Greg Fitzsimmons. It is our understanding that Mr. Fitzsimmons performed services in connection with a show at Walt Disney World on December 30, 1995 through January 1, 1996. We have in our possession a fully-executed agreement for such services pursuant to which Mr. Fitzsimmons was to be paid.

We understand that as of the date hereof, Mr. Fitzsimmons has not yet received such payment. This letter is to inform you that we expect you and your company to honor your contractual obligations. Thus, please forward a check to my attention covering the full amount owed to Mr. Fitzsimmons as soon as possible. If such check is not received by the close of business on September 6, 1996, we intend to take all appropriate steps to protect and enforce Mr. Fitzsimmons's rights under the agreement, including without limitation the institution of litigation seeking, _inter alia_, injunctive relief regarding any use of the results in proceeds of his services, compensatory and punitive damages and attorneys' fees.

Sincerely yours,

Ira Schreck

IS/fmg/8105.IS
cc: Mr. Greg Fitzsimmons

THE CLUBS

RISING STARS

t stand-up comics thrive in the Big Apple. **BY RICH MINTZER**

here's a never-ending wave of stand-up comics taking their well-honed skills to the stages of New York City's comedy clubs. The following seven profiled performers range from the soon-to-be household names to sleeper picks. What separates these few from other numerous rising talents in the city are a) uniqueness of material; b) a persona that just s out. "I'm gonna be a star!"; c) a persistent agent who convinced our writer to o coming back to some hole-in-the-wall West Village club at midnight until the scribe "got" client.

Be that as it may, here's this year's rising Magnificent Seven.

GREG FITZSIMMONS

"New York is so crowded," says Greg Fitzsimmons. "It's important to have an activity to keep your sanity. For me, one night a week — and I do it just on Mondays — I step out into the darkness and take one human life. On Tuesday, the city just feels a little less crowded." OK, so comic Fitzsimmons looks like he was just kicked off "Dawson's Creek" for being over the age limit. But while his boy-next-door image has "sitcom" written all over it, his observational material cuts deeper and has a dark side. Fitzsimmons takes the stage more than 300 nights a year. He is a featured act at all major New York clubs and enjoyed a brief stint hosting the MTV game show "Idiot Savants."

Tarrytown native developing sitcom for Fox TV

By Georgette Gouveia
Staff writer

If Greg Fitzsimmons has his way, Knollwood Country Club in Elmsford will soon be famous on Fox Broadcasting. Sort of.

The 28-year-old comedian, who was raised in Tarrytown and attended public schools there, as well as Rye Country Day School, is developing a new sitcom for Fox based on his experience as a busboy and caddy at Knollwood.

"It will be like 'Taxi,'" the comedy says of that well-remembered sitcom, "a bunch of people who want to do other things. Me, comedy; we just

wants to reality."

Fitzsimmons' gig in Knollwood is a warm-up, along lines best suited for the artist. But you can catch his act Tuesday when he makes his network debut on CBS' "Late Show With David Letterman" (11:35 p.m., Channel 2).

Lately, the media have made much of Letterman's being lampooned in the ratings of Jesse Rochelle's own Jay Leno and his "Tonight Show." For Fitzsimmons, however, Letterman is still tops.

"I always wanted to do Letterman," he says. "It's still the hippest, coolest show. It's definitely the kind of comedy I do — a little bit irreverent, a little

bit silly. The Letterman show is the real deal showcase for bright comedians."

Fitzsimmons' Letterman appearance, at the Ed Sullivan Theater in Manhattan, will be a bittersweet one.

"My dad will be on the show a lot, but in a good way," he says. Fitzsimmons' father, the former Bob Fitzsimmons, died this period. Greg Fitzsimmons also took his best friend. "I've been going to be funny," he says.

Also nice to be on his show. Fitzsimmons might though to see making different way, in his manner. Fitzsimmons, who by says inspires about one-third of his

Greg Fitzsimmons' sitcom is based on his experiences at Knollwood Country Club in Elmsford.

material.

"She provides an edge that she actually lives it," he says.

The comedian himself lives in Manhattan, as does brother Bobby, who's with a band called the Restaurant.

Fitzsimmons believes in keeping comedy in the family. Not only is his mother a source of material but so is dating comedian Sue Costello, who has a deal with CBS to develop her own series. Sounds as if the couple feed both sets on the real career track.

"I manage as if I'd like to take a decent a solid career," he says. "like Sue — Sandy I'd rate about."

Another Hub comic hits Letterman

A nother member of Boston's stand-up community jumps into the major leagues Dec. 26 when Greg Fitzsimmons makes his debut on the "Late Show With David Letterman."

Letterman's show is the Holy Grail for up-and-coming comics. It carries more weight than appearing with Jay Leno on "The Tonight Show," because Letterman doesn't feature stand-ups nearly as often his late-night counterpart.

Letterman's representatives have taken few chances with Fitzsimmons' five-minute network premiere. "They looked at me for

COMEDY
by Dean Johnson

about six months before I got the gig," said Fitzsimmons, who performs tonight and tomorrow at the Comedy Connection in Faneuil Hall. "They kept listening to my stuff and telling me: 'You're going to have to change that word. You can't say that.' So I pretty much already know what I'm going to say. But since I am going to be on the day after Christmas, I'd like to have a few Christmas jokes in there, too."

Fitzsimmons said Letterman's reps were losing interest in him about the time of the Just for Laughs festival in Montreal in July. But they were impressed with his sets there and gave him a

second look.

Who'll be the next Boston comic to hit the jackpot in Montreal? The answer may be at the Comedy Connection on Sunday night. Just for Laughs reps will be taking in the Connection's 7 p.m. showcase to check out Hub talent and see if any of the comics are ready to make the leap to next summer's bash.

The lineup will include Kevin Knox, Paul D'Angelo, Ed Regine, Jim Dunn, Tom Cotter, Jim Lauletta, Chris McGuire and Al Ducharme, with others to be added.

Sunday's audience will also include ABC-TV casting folks on the lookout for people to join the ensemble crew of Dana Carvey's untitled new show.

"Mass Hysteria!," the musical

THE SHOW BUSINESS

BY JENNY JEDEIKIN

No Laughing Matter

For aspiring comic stars, the Just for Laughs Festival isn't just for laughs

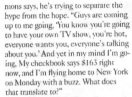

TWO WEEKS BEFORE LANDING A last-minute gig at the Just for Laughs Festival in Montreal, things weren't going so well for 29-year-old comedian Greg Fitzsimmons. He was let go from his job writing for *Politically Incorrect*, he was having trouble getting the folks at *Letterman* to give him a booking, and, although he'd been in the business seven years, he still wasn't signed with an agency. Midway through the festival, Fitzsimmons took the stage of the Comedy Nest and reeled off the first line of his set: "I have seven minutes to turn around a seven-year career slump." He wasn't kidding. After charming the audience with his carefully crafted material, made more endearing by his boyishly freckled face, Fitzsimmons exited the stage, only to be approached immediately by a woman from William Morris. "Don't look now," she told him, "but there's a line of agents and network people behind me waiting to talk to you."

If you tune in to Fox's *Just for Laughs* festival Saturday night, you'll see a show hosted by *Friends*' David Schwimmer and the familiar clips from a cavalcade of stand-ups turned sitcom stars, some of whom got their break at the festival. What you won't see is the lion's share of what goes on behind the scenes: the network reps and Hollywood agents scrambling to cultivate and groom the new, unfettered talent to ensure healthy product for the next crop of sitcoms.

"They want you to be raw and undeveloped," says Fitzsimmons two days after his killer set. "The networks and agents are looking for someone they haven't seen before so they can go back to Hollywood and go, 'We discovered so and so.'" The newly discovered New York native is in the lobby of the Delta Hotel—where the industry camps out until the wee hours of the morning—and he's busy acquiring a new skill: avoiding people. "I feel like a pinball bouncing off people," he says. "Every network has come up to me. I had a manager talk to me for 15 minutes, blow smoke up my a—, tell me how great I was and then say, 'I'm looking forward to seeing your act tomorrow.'" At this moment, Fitzsimmons says, he's trying to separate the hype from the hope. "Guys are coming up to me going, 'You know you're going to have your own TV show, you're hot, everyone wants you, everyone's talking about you.' And yet in my mind I'm going, My checkbook says $163 right now, and I'm flying home to New York on Monday with a buzz. What does that translate to?"

Fitzsimmons is hoping, of course, that all this will translate into a bona fide development deal with a major network. Because even for the tried-and-true comic, there is nothing at the end of the road-weary nightclub-filled line quite so golden. Even Richard Lewis—in town to do a tribute to John Candy—gets defensive when sitcom deals are mentioned (and he once had a hit with *Anything but Love*). "I came here to be a comedian again," he says abruptly. "I didn't come here to audition." But after prodding, Lewis will concede that he, too, wishes he could meet his own Larry David. "I want to do a sitcom," says Lewis, "but only if it's according to my sensibilities. My agents are looking for a producer who wants to work with me, who understands my head." And David Brenner is quick to cough up stories about having had ideas for shows that are now hit series, such as a show about "behind the scenes of a TV talk show." "I have yet to meet a programming development person that was deep," says Brenner, who came to the festival with his syndicated radio show. "If I'd met one, I'd have a hit show."

Still, the coveted deal, in which a network offers money to the comic in exchange for his or her commitment to a future project, is no guarantee of landing on the air. At Comedy Central's late-night party at the

PAUL CORIO

The New York Times

Sunday, March 9, 1997

ARTS AND LEISURE DESK

A Comic Races to Stay in Place

By NEIL STRAUSS

"WANT TO SEE something funny?" Greg Fitzsimmons asks. It better be funny, because funny is Mr. Fitzsimmons's business. He is currently New York comedy's golden boy. And right now he is standing in a USA Network editing suite examining "Temporarily Fitzsimmons," a segment he does for "USA Live" in which he experiences life in a new workplace every week. This time, he spent eight hours as an employee in a grocery store. The result: Four very funny minutes of cable television.

Mr. Fitzsimmons pushes through the door of the editing suite and takes three steps across a hall. In the next room, his face grins from six different television sets. It's not a USA Network room, however. It's command central for "Idiot Savants," a quirky MTV quiz show for which he is the host.

These days, Mr. Fitzsimmons is all over television. Yet almost every night, he is also out pounding the pavement, running from comedy club to comedy club, performing for as little as $10 a routine. On television, he makes slightly more than $100,000 a year (before agent's and manager's fees). But that's a paltry figure compared with the money being thrown at comics at places like last week's United States Comedy Arts Festival in Aspen, Colo.

The previous week, Mr. Fitzsimmons, 30, had tried to break a local comedy record by performing in 10 different comedy clubs in one night. He only made it to eight. On this night he has it easy: only four clubs are on his agenda, although at one of them he will do an audition for a second appearance on "Late Show With David Letterman."

As Mr. Fitzsimmons leaves the building to begin the night's comedy trek, an older, distinguished-looking man comes up to him. "I just wanted to say that you're a genius," he says. "An absolute pure genius. If there's ever anything I can do for you, just let me know."

Who was that? A powerful network executive? "A USA cameraman," Mr. Fitzsimmons says with a sigh. "The only people who come up to me and say things like that are flunkies and middle-aged women. Never beautiful young girls."

The most impressive one to me (and my mother) came from her old workplace, *The New York Times*. A two-page profile by Neil Strauss detailed the precarious situation I was in as a comedian trying to juggle a lot of balls at once.

movie-review segment for a new show on Comedy Central. While taping a scene where we walk though Times Square, as a joke, we pretended to make fun of this new show. We were wearing microphones and cracking up the sound guy, since we knew the dialogue was not going to be used.

Two days later, our manager called to say that the executive producer of the show had heard what we said and axed us from the show. When we told him we were just goofing around, he assured us that the producer would be fine with us if we just called her and apologized. Ross and I agreed that if this woman lacked the sense of humor to see that we were kidding around in the first place, there was no reason to waste our time making the call; the show was doomed. Who the hell was going to watch something called *The Daily Show* anyway?

Even the Friars Club, a place that had been a big part of my life, became a source of drama. Each year, the Friars invited my family to their infamous roasts where I sat in awe of legends like Alan King, Milton Berle, Shecky Greene, and Henny Youngman. I'd been going since I was a teenager dreaming of one day sitting on the dais. The thrill of being a spectator turned to frustration as I was passed over as a performer each year. I now had substantial credits but felt that the Friars Club would never really see me as anyone but my father's son. I became increasingly hurt and rejected as I saw other comedians join the club and enjoy the praise and acceptance of the Friars community that I felt I was not getting. Eventually, I stopped going to the club completely. It felt like an extension of my father: exciting and important, yet a place from which I could not get any real acceptance.

One thing I did not miss was the nudity. The Friar's Club has the best steam room in the city. I would work out and then relax on the marble benches, chatting with the old guys and sweating. After showering, I would put a towel around my waist. The eighty-year-old members preferred letting it all hang out (and down). They walked around powdering their balls and farting and then powdering their ass and then coughing up phlegm. Their penises (or is it peni?) seemed to be melting towards the floor and I struggled to avert my eyes but some part of me needed to know what I would look like in another fifty years. It's not something I look forward to.

This self-imposed exile from the club was a further reminder that, as I

COMEDY

PLAYING THE GAME

Greg Fitzsimmons knows hosting MTV's *Idiot Savants* is a good gig. But he doesn't have to be happy about it.

When you're smiling: host Greg Fitzsimmons.

See the telegenic man in the photo above? That's comedian Greg Fitzsimmons, host of *Idiot Savants*, MTV's latest hip game show. Looks happy to be him, doesn't he? Well, it's just because he's a professional, not because he's glad to be a game-show personality. After seven years of crafting his stand-up act and writing for the likes of *Politically Incorrect*, this was not necessarily the showcase 30-year-old Fitzsimmons had in mind. Being a well-scrubbed TV face is a little awkward when it doesn't match your dark outlook, and today Fitzsimmons is all mouth. Maybe he has softened up from the therapy session that preceded this interview—or it could be he's looking for trouble because he's bored playing it safe.

Time Out New York: Your father, [the late] Bob Fitzsimmons, was huge in talk radio for 25 years, so I guess hosting runs in the family. Did his career influence you?

Greg Fitzsimmons: It had a huge effect on my approach to the business. My father was a guy who went years without radio jobs sometimes. He would do voice-overs in between], and over time, I saw he was very successful. I mean he was an upper-middle-class guy who did it in a business where most people think you either make it big or you don't make it all. He was a hustler, a great schmoozer and very well liked. A lot of that rubbed off on me.

TONY: You're a pragmatist, then?

GF: I sort of straddle wanting to be commercially successful and also knowing that it doesn't really make me happy. It's not about the money as much as it is about succeeding—or more specifically, not failing. In a way, I feel it's a cop-out that my approach is more businesslike than a lot of people's. I've always felt that nothing I have accomplished so far is worth shit. It's all about taking that and

parlaying it to the next level. Like being at a roulette wheel and whatever you win, putting it back on the table. Because this is all fucking bullshit.

TONY: What's bullshit?

GF: Hosting a game show, first of all, is something I was totally against. My manager basically talked me into doing it. Part of me knows it was a chess move, to get experience in front of the camera, to get a little buzz going on. As long as you remember the whole business is a game and the stakes are just as imaginary as one of those fake poker nights. Because as soon as you invest your self-esteem in the fruits of what you get from this business, you're completely fucked, because it is random.

TONY: What made you run all over town last Saturday night trying to do ten sets in one night? Are you that needy?

GF: Extremely. I don't think there's a comedian out there who's not. Making people laugh, it's all I have. I've always had the void. And of all my addictions, comedy is probably the healthiest.

TONY: You don't seem very happy.

GF: I think if you want to make a comedian really unhappy, give him some success. I don't think there's anything wrong with the game show; I think it's all in my head. The process was really fun, and I stand by the show. It's no more contrived than any sitcom out there.

I said a long time ago, "I'm never going to host a game show," because I knew I was a candidate for that. I've always defied being stereotyped in any way.

TONY: Do you defy through your material? Have you been acting out more since Idiot Savants?

GF: I hope so. Since the game show, I've noticed my reaction has been to be much more profane onstage. It's just lashing out; it's just sabotage in some way.

TONY: Four years ago, if you had imagined yourself being in this position—on TV regularly, as a headliner, your name in the paper—would you have thought it would make you happy?

GF: Yeah. But nothing's ever really made me happy. Doing *Letterman* made me happy. Stand-up fulfills me. When people compliment me on my stand-up, I feel really good; when they compliment me on the game show, I just want to turn around and walk away.

TONY: Here's a quote I read recently from Stewart Lee, a British comic: "Comedians know they are only lazy chancers, talented idlers, wimps, losers, bullshitters and con men." Agree or disagree?

GF: I agree with that. I mean, who isn't? Everybody's bullshittin' everybody. Everything's a con, and everybody wants a take. I just think it's funny that people credit [comedians]. They'll go, "Well, you should feel good, you're making people laugh." And it's, like, that's the furthest thing from my mind, that I'm making somebody laugh. It's all about me. It's completely a selfish act. I'm taking from them. I'm not there to fucking give. I could care less. All the things I've given up, all the relationships on the side of the road to get there—what, to make strangers feel better? Fuck that. It's like a hooker saying, "I just want to make people feel good."
—*Cynthia Truu*

Greg Fitzsimmons will be at Caroline's March 13 through 16, where, despite his intentions, he will make you laugh.

MTV won't suffer 'Idiot'

NEW YORK — MTV takes constant ribbing within the industry for almost never canceling a show — "Beavis & Butt-head" and "Real World" seem to go on forever.

So cable mavens took notice when the cable net decided not to pick up the option for another 65 half-hour episodes of "Idiot Savants," the nightly quiz show.

The show kicked off as a double-run five-a-weeker on Dec. 9 at 7 p.m. and 11 p.m. Most recently, MTV was running it every weeknight at 7:30.

The creators of the show were Michael Dugan and Chris Kreski. Dugan, who also wrote and produced "Idiot," is MTV's VP of development, and Kreski is the network's editorial director. An MTV spokeswoman said the show will probably continue in reruns.

had been told as a child, I needed to get my attitude in check. This was not the person that I knew I was or wanted to be. I was in a clichéd trap of success and what was underneath it was that I didn't care about anything. I was really just scared, but it came out as resentment and it was often unjustified.

It pained me as I looked back over my relationship with the Friars Club and saw what an amazing part of my life it had always been. The fall after my dad passed I'd begun acting school and spent a lot of time at the clubhouse shooting pool, working out, and talking with the guys I've known since I was a kid. People there knew my family well and my father better. I was looked after and made to feel like I was welcome every time I went in. It was a powerful bridge to my father at a time I really needed one.

My father had eaten lunch at the club the day he died. Twenty-seven different people told me during the wake that they had eaten with him that day. That obviously cannot be true, but that's how people felt about my father; like they had just been with him. It was the one place where I never saw my father in a bad mood. He'd been embraced by the mostly Jewish

I bet any kid who was forced to learn Irish step dancing has a book in him darker and more interesting than mine.

membership as their token Irish guy. He threw a Saint Patrick's Day party in the Milton Berle Room every year for as long as I can remember. He'd sport this lime-green jacket that looked like he'd just won the Masters Golf Tournament and bring in traditional Irish step dancers.

The party attracted friends from the worlds of radio and commercials, as well as close friends and family. It became a tradition that my mother and I would get up and sing an old Irish ballad called "Four Green Fields." By the end, there would not be a dry eye in the house. It was that bad. People laughed hysterically from the first off-key note to the last disharmonizing verse.

My father was very active in the club, and he went on to be a board member and eventually the scribe. I spent a lot of Saturdays at the Friars Club brunch, and during senior year of high school, the students were given a chance to get experience in whatever field interested them most. I wanted to be a comedy writer, so my father introduced me to some of his good friends from the club. They generously took me into their world. Freddie Roman picked me up in his Cadillac and drove me up to a resort in the Catskills so I could see a professional do it from beginning to end. I can still remember jokes from that night: "If you don't know what a schmuck is, he's a guy that gets out of the shower to pee."

I saw Freddie take a group of distracted people who appeared too old to understand the jokes—let alone hear and see them—and corral, shape, and delight them. He wore a crisp tuxedo and delivered every joke with the salesmanship of a maître d' at a five-star restaurant. He was neither nervous before the show nor visibly different afterward. It was simply what he did.

Years later, when I moved to New York, Freddie would sponsor me as a member in the club and years after that would introduce me to his son, Alan Kirschenbaum, a very successful TV writer in Los Angeles. My father asked Freddie to emcee a charity golf tournament he'd started at the Friars Club, and Freddie, as always, agreed. When my father passed away, they named the tournament after him, and Freddie continues to produce and emcee the event to this day.

My other mentor from the club was the famous *Saturday Night Live* writer Alan Zweibel. Alan was one of the original writers and created classic bits like Rosanne Roseannadanna, Emily Litella, and the killer bees. Alan was generous enough to read scripts I was writing for a cable-access show and invite me to events in the city. At seventeen years old, I found myself at a book party in cast member Gilda Radner's apartment. Gilda teased me about looking like I should've been in bed hours before, and I got to meet other *SNL* cast members. I saw that Alan and Gilda had a very close, very special relationship in which she never let him leave her side. She was fragile yet joyful. He understood her, and they had a lifelong friendship which, after she died, he captured beautifully in his book *Bunny Bunny*.

The Friars seemed like an extension of my family. My parents dined there often, and we celebrated events there as if it were our second living room. I can remember the insane celebration of watching the U.S. Olympic hockey team defeat the Soviet team in 1980 on the giant TV at the club. I can remember years later gathering around that same television with a group of men in shock as police cars pursued O.J. Simpson's white Ford Bronco through Los Angeles.

One of the last times I went to the club was to attend the swearing-in ceremony for a friend of mine, Sarah Fearon, whom I'd sponsored as a member. I'd spent about twenty minutes talking to a friend that she'd brought along named Erin. I pulled Sarah aside later to tell her that I would be marrying Erin someday. On mine and Erin's first date, I walked her home on Bowery Street, where a homeless man sang "Unforgettable" to us for a dollar. We danced in the street, and I knew this was it.

Prior to meeting Erin, I'd been in a couple of long-term relationships that did not end well. Erin's calm energy immediately attracted me to her. She also has a spectacular rack. I remember not being able to figure her out. (I still can't.) She had every reason in the world to be angry and defiant after having grown up in the middle of her parents' ugly divorce. But nothing fazed her, including me, although I kept testing her.

Early in our relationship, I invited her up to a gig in the Adirondack Mountains. The hotel was moldy and gross. The show was in a tin roadhouse in front of a group of townies who were still drunk from last week's show. I bombed, but mostly because karaoke night followed the comedy, and they were getting restless. Roger, who owned the "club," had walked his wife home and now returned wearing a dress, high heels, and a wig. He hosted karaoke night as his alter ego, "Giselle." His wife, according to people we

The captain wore sunglasses because he didn't like how his mascara had turned out.

met, had no idea Giselle existed. Giselle insisted that we meet her (or would it be him?) at six the next morning to deliver the mail. Roger/Giselle wore a third hat in town and delivered the mail via motorboat dock-to-dock all around the lake. He'd expertly swerve in close enough to toss and catch mailbags with the residents, without getting so close that they'd notice his faded lipstick and rouge from the night before. Erin loved Roger, and I loved Erin.

Another excellent opportunity Erin missed to get out of the relationship happened on our way to an IKEA store in New Jersey. After being cut off by a guy who apologized by giving me the finger, I moved up ahead of him and then very artfully drove him off the road onto the shoulder. As the ant that had just crashed our little picnic tried in vain to make his way back onto the highway, Erin began giggling. I figured there must be something wrong with her. In reality I think she had grown up in a world that was serious and she was now having fun.

I never felt judged by Erin or pressured to reign in my childish sense of humor. I didn't cower when I'd done something wrong and I didn't fantasize about getting out of the relationship when she asked something of me. Becoming deeply involved with a woman without making her my boss or me hers was disorienting. I'm still not really used to it, but I am forever grateful for her. Erin is one of the most truthful, pure people I've ever known, and it's been fourteen years now. I think she's going to snap real bad one day soon.

For the first three years, our courtship was interrupted constantly by my road work and week-long trips to Los Angeles for meetings and auditions. Our decision to move to Los Angeles marked my belief that I would one day skyrocket to the middle regions of show business. It also signified Erin's belief in my career and in our relationship. At thirty years old, she had never lived off the island of Manhattan. She was working in the film world and had often pictured herself one day living in LA. But before we left New York, there was something that needed to be done.

On Erin's birthday I took her to the Friars Club, where I hadn't been in years. We walked into a place so romantic most girls only dream of it: the Milton Berle Room! The manager, Michael Caputo, arranged to have our song, "Unforgettable," playing, and as we danced I gazed over at the portraits of all the legendary members on the wall, including the late Bob Fitzsimmons. I asked Erin to marry me. She cried but did not answer. (I imagine she'd been hoping for a better location and a better man.)

Standing there waiting for a reply I knew that this spot was more than just sentimental. I would not start a family if I was not sure that I could handle it; every aspect of it. The Friars Club was a place where I'd gotten stuck, and I knew that being a good father and a good husband meant fighting your way out of "stuck," even when it is painful. Being here meant I was going to give it my best shot.

With Erin having still not answered, I hustled her off to dinner and a Broadway show, figuring she was into the marriage thing. We met our friends at the King Cole Bar at the St. Regis Hotel for a drink and then took a carriage ride through the falling snow in Central Park. I threw a move on her as we clomped past Strawberry Fields, but she shut me down. I felt that was an insult to John Lennon, but I married her anyway. Thinking back, I should have gone Asian.

Did I cry? Let's just say that I recognized the priest who performed the vows and leave it at that.

I know what you're wondering: how did a sober, hostile comedian living in a void left by the loss of his father (and primary authority figure) meet a nice woman and start a normal family? Let's just say this "nice woman" may not have turned out to be so "nice" after all . . .

The Perfect Woman and the Man Who Will One Day Destroy Her

Rebellion without truth is like spring in a bleak, arid desert.

—Kahlil Gibran

Just kidding about Erin not being "nice" at the end of chapter ten. I couldn't think of a good cliff-hanger ending and so I threw that in. She's actually very nice to the point of being annoying. Erin grew up on the Upper West Side of Manhattan back when the Upper West Side of Manhattan was not yet the Upper West Side of Manhattan. Her father, Joel Kovel, is a left-wing intellectual who ran for president in 2000 and was on Fidel Castro's invite list at the UN about six years ago.

Joel was raised "not-Jewish" by Russian Jewish parents in a gang of nerds including none other than Woody Allen (who had a different name back then because he was still Jewish).

Not fully understanding Joel's explanation of why his dad was not in step with his neighbors, suffice it to say Joel was born into defiance. At a time when it was difficult for a Jew to even get in to Yale, Joel graduated in the top 3 percent of his class. After getting his medical degree, Joel met Erin's mother, Virginia, at Albert Einstein College of Medicine in the Bronx.

An Irish Catholic from that borough, Virginia worked as a nurse. Erin's mother and my mother both went to the same high school (they did not know each other), and that is where the two women's similarities end.

Joel Kovel

U.S. Senator • N.Y. '98
Green Party of New York State

for the people
for the earth

for the future of our children
for the children of our future

Okay, the Green Party never wins. But it's still cool that my father-in-law ran for senator and then president on their ticket.

Pulling out an old yearbook from St. Benedict's High School, my aunts tease my mother-in-law, Virginia, about her yearbook page: debate club, French club, penmanship club. My mother and her sisters seem to have participated in almost no activities while in high school. It may have been the school's fault for not scheduling any directly behind the school, where they were sneaking off to smoke cigarettes and fool around with boys.

Virginia's family brought a whole different basket of dysfunction to the picnic. Virginia was a "surprise from God" baby; her mother was forty-seven when she got pregnant with her. Ashamed by the pregnancy and severely depressed by her eldest son's death, Virginia's mom gave her little support early in life.

When Joel and Virginia married, most of the members of their families did not attend their interfaith wedding. It might have been the couple's strategy from the beginning to escape their families. They divorced when Erin was about thirteen and she was raised mostly by her mother. Erin was born on December 23, two days before the Lord Jesus Christ. I had way more respect for her parents after realizing that they had participated in the traditional Saint Patrick's Day Fornication Ceremony.

A latchkey kid, Erin was hanging around dives in the East Village decades before all of the posers turned it into Disney for trust fund kids. She drifted around—at one point overseeing the library of a porn producer, then working at a homeless shelter in Harlem for men with AIDS while getting her master's degree in social work at Columbia University.

When I met Erin, she was working for a major movie star, attending premieres and parties at night and working in plush offices downtown during the day. Having a boyfriend who told jokes to drunk tourists eating chicken wings didn't impress her (or anyone, now that I think about it). She was drawn to the fact that I was honest, had quit drinking, and was going after what I wanted in life. From the beginning, Erin has always loved the concept of me; I don't know that she's ever been that interested in the details. She loves me for who I am. When I try to ask her who I am she will not tell me, but she loves me. I don't look for her to approve of what I do and in turn, I more often than not behave like an adult.

Sometimes she even gets involved with my stupidity, like when we were having trouble getting out of our gym membership.

The note on the next page prompted me to start digging through the letters I'd only remembered as negative to see if there were more helpful ones mixed in. There were! An encouraging note from the principal of Rye County Day was sent from a teacher who'd taken the time to send me this in the middle of the summer.

Being in Hollywood now was bringing out the worst in me, and I was blowing a lot of opportunities by trying to show people that I didn't need them. I've been fortunate enough to have many talented and hard-working Jewish people set up hundreds of opportunities for me to audition for jobs. I would imagine most of them have been fired.

1253 26th Street # B   [Jan. 18, 2001
Santa Monica, CA 90404

To whom it may concern

My wife and I wish to terminate our membership at Bally Total Fitness at this point.

(Greg Fitzsimmons/Erin Kovel: Contract # 0042894899014
Joined on Jan. 25, 1998 @ 641 Ave. of Americas, NYC, 10011 by employee #691640.
Our previous address was 54 w. 16 street #5F, NYC 10011. Enclosed are copies of our
original contract as well as your official "Notice of Cancellation" form)

We have paid for three years of this membership even though we have not gone to the
club for the past year and a half. We were not allowed out of the contract when we
wanted to be after having been assured by the sales person that it would not be a problem.
He also told us it was a 2 year contract, and although it is our fault for not examining the
lengthy contract more thoroughly, it did not occur to us that a corporation the size of
Ballys was in the business of locking people into iron-clad unbreakable contracts against
their will. This is a health club, not a student loan or a mortgage.

I could go on, but suffice to say we have now held up our end of the agreement and spent
over $1000.00 over the last year and a half because of your company's ridiculous
inflexibility. Normally I would assume that the termination date on a contract would
mean exactly that. However with Ballys Total Fitness, it may mean you automatically
sign me up for another three years at a higher rate and our child must join as well. Let
me make myself clear. We want out. If there are any complications, I will do the
following:

1) Write a letter to the Better Business Bureau
2) I'm sure you are familiar with a New York Post article detailing the horrendous way
   you have treated unsuspecting members including cancer patients and invalids who
   were held to their contracts. I have made copies of this and will post them at the
   Ballys near my house daily. I will also hand them to anybody I see on a guest tour of
   the club.
3) As a nationally touring comedian, I will make a point of doing material nightly about
   your club and then doing the material on ALL of the many network television
   appearances I make.

Thank you for your time.

Sincerely,

Greg Fitzsimmons   Erin Kovel-Fitzsimmons

Dear Mrs. Fitzsimmons

And we got a response:

Bally Total Fitness
300 East Joppa Road
Baltimore, MD 21286-3020

```
#BWNBNWT K01
*0042894899006 0A  0*  BTF 8 NY
ERIN KOVEL
1253 26TH ST # B
SANTA MONICA CA  90404-1403
```
                                                              02-07-2001

RE: Account Number: 0042894899006

Dear Erin Kovel,

This letter confirms that your health club membership has been cancelled. Bally Total Fitness is sorry to see you leave and hopes that we may be of service sometime in the future.

If you have any questions, please feel free to contact us.

Sincerely,

Bally Total Fitness
Member Services
1-410-296-1950

Office Hours:
9AM-5:30PM EASTERN
MONDAY-FRIDAY
www.ballyfitness.com

K01
2701
A   2210

> Dear Bug,
>
> This is just a note to remind you that I would like to display your sculpture in my office during this school year.
>
> I hope that you've had a good summer and that 1982–83 will be your best year at RCDS.
>
> See you soon.
>
> Sincerely,
> James P. Godfrey
>
> 8/16/82

For me, being funny was always in reaction to somebody telling me what to do, whether it was a teacher, a parent, or a crowd of people in a comedy club. This dynamic did not lend itself to high-pressure situations. My favorite audition of all time happened about ten years ago when I was sent in on a brand-new show called *Veronica's Closet*. My agent told me that the character I was going in for was gay, but the producer didn't want the actors to play it gay. Not understanding what the fuck that could possibly mean, I simply read the lines the way I normally would. When I finished, the casting director jumped up excitedly and said, "That was great! Try it again, but a little less gay." Not able to dig in and just give a manlier read, I mailed it in and went home to bitch to my wife about my agent.

If my audition skills didn't kill my chances, my chronic lateness did. After winning the Jury Prize for Best Comedian at the 2001 HBO Comedy Arts Festival in Aspen, the heat was back. A meeting was scheduled at NBC with not only the head of every department but with the president of NBC, Jeff

June 17

Dear Greg,
Your note was one of the bright spots in what has been otherwise a somewhat difficult season — my final term at RCDS. It is high time that I left high school, and I am off next month to a new position at a brand-new, high-tech, private day school down in North Carolina, a whole set of fresh challenges at just the time when I need to do something

different.
I remember you very well — and would even without the NYTimes article which I clipped and passed around at school. Who could forget that you renamed the major characters in Hardy's *Return of the Native* Clam and Crustacea? The English Department couldn't take the book seriously after that and had to drop it.
I had forgotten, though, about the dinner jacket. Wear it in good health. I'll be watching on 7/2.

Morrow Jones

Zucker. The heat became lukewarm when I was twenty minutes late for the meeting. It was ice-cold when I strolled in ten minutes after that. They did, however, still validate my parking.

It was starting to feel familiar. I had to stop and remind myself where this shitty attitude would lead. Being defiant was not getting me anywhere and I had a wife and son now counting on me. I wanted to be a man about this even if being a man in my case meant double-checking my directions to "The Comedy Fart Trap" in Sacramento. It wasn't enough to just pay the bills now either. I had the extra pressure of trying to live up to my promise of not punching out on the family along the way. Like Popeye needs his spinach for strength, I needed a goddamn letter from someone! It came from an old teacher of mine from Rye Country Day. Morrow Jones was the creative writing teacher who had suggested I do comedy for a living. Now he was writing to tell me he was proud that I had done it.

I'd spent four years of my life viewing these teachers as my oppressors, but I now saw that they had been my saviors. Somehow Mr. Godfrey and Mr. Robertson (the principal and the Dean of Boys) had seen past the horrible grades and worse behavior. They really cared about me.

Mrs. Fitzsimmons –

We have certainly enjoyed Greg the short time he's been in our class. I truly admire his individual spirit and hope he's able to retain this throughout his school year.

Happy Summer –
Mrs. Johnson

The teacher who was once critical of my wiggling seemed to have ended the year with encouragement.

Dear Mr. & Mrs. Fitzsimmons:

Even though these reports are a week stale now, I thought you would like to see them. Mr. Brown is still worried about three courses: biology, math, and French. I hope that the math tutoring is helping; that we should see fairly soon.

I had just a brief chat with Greg yesterday. He is not happy with the school, but he still smiles when he says it. It must hurt him terribly. And it hurts us as well to see someone we know to be bright not making the grade academically. He looks diligent; no one complains too much about work not being handed in; and yet the results aren't there. I sincerely hope that we can pull him out of his difficulties; if not, we are failing somewhat too.

Sincerely,

Glen Robertson
Glen Robertson
Dean of Boys

10/16/80

I Wouldn't Be Where I Am Today
(Where the Hell Am I?)

> . . . This is not my beautiful house . . . This is not my beautiful wife.
>
> —Talking Heads

I was being summoned to the dais. The Friars were honoring a guy I had always looked up to: Pat Cooper. My family sat out in the Hilton ballroom and watched as I tore him a new asshole—just like I was one of the guys. If a younger version of me resented that the Friars could only see me as my father's son, now I was proud of that distinction. I was comfortable up there, which is something I realized I had never felt while in front of crowds at other Friars Club events.

I started replacing a lot of my road work around this time with TV writing jobs. I spent more time with my family and learned a lot about producing from some very talented people. I've been lucky enough to work with Cedrick the Entertainer, Louis C.K., Dave Attell, Chelsea Handler, and many more. As one of the original producers and writers on *The Ellen DeGeneres Show*, I won four Daytime Emmys.

Along the way I was hosting or acting in at least two pilots a year and spent about four years making fun of bad TV shows on VH1's *Best Week Ever* (please hold your ironic punch lines).

During this time I was becoming a regular on *The Howard Stern Radio Show*. A fixture on the show, Jackie "The Jokeman" Martling had left and I

THE NATIONAL ACADEMY
OF TELEVISION ARTS & SCIENCES

Honors

GREG FITZSIMMONS, Producer

For the Emmy Award-Winning Program

The Ellen DeGeneres Show

SYNDICATED

The 32nd Annual

DAYTIME EMMY® AWARDS

May 20, 2006

HERBERT A. GRANATH
CHAIRMAN
THE NATIONAL ACADEMY OF
TELEVISION ARTS & SCIENCES

FRANK J. RADICE
PRESIDENT
THE NATIONAL ACADEMY OF
TELEVISION ARTS & SCIENCES

was brought in as a possible replacement. The job, rightfully, went to Artie Lange. Artie had been a friend of mine before joining the Stern gang, and was always a champion of mine when I would come into the studio. Although Howard has turned out to be extremely supportive of me, the first time I came in was one of the scariest experiences of my life.

The backstory between Stern and my dad made me apprehensive about being there in the first place. I had become a fan of the show later in life, but it was a guilty pleasure as my mom, to this day, cannot bear to hear Howard's name mentioned. Howard's attacks on my father were mitigated by the on-air eulogy he delivered about him upon hearing he'd passed. He described him as one of the most-liked people in radio. He was respectful and generous in honoring my dad's memory and that meant a lot to me. That being said, this was still *The Howard Stern Show* and my defenses were up based on what I'd heard the week before.

The show was in repeats the week prior to my coming in. One of the episodes that reran contained a diatribe against my father from at least ten years before. I froze up thinking that this whole thing was a set-up. I found

LOS ANGELES TIMES

Howard Stern Still Seeking a Joke Man

Comics seem to be auditioning for key spot vacated by Jackie Martling, who left after a contract dispute.

Associated Press

Jackie "The Joke Man" Martling, left, and Howard Stern in 1998.

Around the Dial

By PAUL BROWNFIELD
TIMES STAFF WRITER

Stand-up comedians need radio exposure, particularly the kind offered by "The Howard Stern Radio Show." In addition to Stern's sizable reach (at least 8.5 million listeners over the course of a week, according to the radio industry publication Talkers magazine), there is also the stamp of approval from Stern, who has the kind of clout to make an endorsement meaningful. Ask touring comics about promotion, and chances are they've been on end-

less local "morning zoo" shows, doing two minutes of material to tease that weekend's club dates.

Unlike television, there are fewer opportunities to reach chunks of the country at once. Comics go on "The Bob and Tom Show," the morning-drive show syndicated out of Indianapolis, to reach Middle America. But it doesn't beat exposure on "Stern."

So when Jackie "The Joke Man" Martling, Stern's resident comic and joke writer, left the show in a contract dispute in March, comics and managers smelled an opportunity. Though the show—heard locally on KLSX-FM (97.1) and syndicated by Viacom-owned Infinity

Broadcasting Corp.—hasn't presented their appearances as such, numerous comics seem to be auditioning for Martling's role.

Stern indicated on the air this week that Martling wouldn't be back. In his place, the young,

anointed ones have included comedians Doug Stanhope, Craig Gass, Greg Fitzsimmons and Jeffrey Ross.

"Howard now has the opportunity to cast out to see what other

Please see Radio, F27

FRIDAY, APRIL 27, 2001   **F27**

Radio: Comic Fed Stern One-Liners on the Fly

Continued from F2

elements may work on the show," said Don Buchwald, Stern's long-time agent. "We've culled a list of people, some comics, some writers, some voice people who have been participating on the show."

They aren't exactly household names, but neither was Martling when Stern enlisted his services in 1983, shortly before the radio personality's move from Washington, D.C., to New York and gradual ascension to "King of All Media"-hood. Martling was along for the ride, part of Stern's comedy circus, an encyclopedic teller of off-color jokes and plugger of stand-up dates at places like Governor's comedy club on Long Island.

What fewer listeners realized was that Martling was also writing material for Stern—one-liners he would hastily print on a piece of paper with a Sharpie pen. Martling says he would then put the paper under a camera lens so that the gags and messages would appear on Stern's monitor. Sometimes Stern ignored the jokes, sometimes he used them—the point was to get them up there, to feed the Stern maw. "Flying gag writer" is what Martling called himself.

"As far as I know, I invented it, not that there's any great invention to it," Martling said. ". . . I don't remember ever seeing pictures of Bob Hope talking on radio and someone handing him notes as he went along. He was reading from a script."

Martling, 53, got on the phone with the media this week to promote his appearance on "Son of the Beach," the "Baywatch" parody on cable's FX network. It's a low-rated series, but it has Stern's name on it (he's executive producer), and Stern has made ample use of his airwaves to talk about how fantastic the show is. Stern's radio show, in fact, has increasingly become less a show than a PR platform for his TV pro-

duction arm, whether it's "Son of the Beach" or his late-night shows on CBS and E! Entertainment Television or an animated series, "Doomsday," that has been in development either at UPN for several years.

Martling, for his part, seemed to be yearning for a return to his former radio family. "Everybody keeps e-mailing me and saying, 'Why don't you compromise?' " he said.

Martling declined to discuss financial specifics, although it is believed the sides were at odds over six-figure proposals. "We were ready to keep negotiating. . . . But what do you do? What card do I have to play? I have one card, and that's [to] stay home."

Martling isn't just staying

> "We were ready to keep negotiating. . . . But what do you do? What card do I have to play? I have one card, and that's [to] stay home."
>
> **JACKIE MARTLING**
> *Former resident comic and joke writer on "The Howard Stern Radio Show."*

home—he's still on the road and pushing his latest CD. "F. Jackie" ("I just did a show at Trump Marina [in Atlantic City]. It wasn't advertised on the Stern show, and we sold out 1,600 seats," Martling boasted.

Becoming part of Stern's world is not a position gained easily. Like Martling, Stanhope, says Judi Brown, his manager, had been sending his material to the show for a year and a half before Stern began playing a suicide bit from Stanhope's CD, "A Little Something to Take the Edge Off." Stanhope's Sam Kinison-esque subjects—sex, death and midgets, to name three—evidently helped rec-

ommend him. He has sat in during the show twice, an honor that for today's comic is something akin to Johnny Carson's coveted "waveover," wherein Carson invited certain comics to sit down with him after their "Tonight Show" sets went well.

Doing well on Stern's show, Brown and others say, doesn't involve polishing your best six minutes. It involves understanding Stern's rhythms, the fact that he's not looking for material so much as a personality with whom he can mesh.

"Howard is amazing to watch work," said Ron Zimmerman, a comic and writer who has known Stern for more than 20 years and has been a writer-in-residence on the show in recent weeks. To see Stern work, Zimmerman says, is to understand how seamlessly he blends disparate voices and comedic elements. Zimmerman likens it to a bandleader. "Howard is like Duke Ellington. Everybody is an instrument in the orchestra that is 'The Howard Stern Show.' "

Lately, says Zimmerman, who lives in L.A., he and Stern have been informally brainstorming on-air bits via phone calls and e-mails. "We have very similar senses of humor about show business and women," he said.

Martling's departure comes at a time when "The Howard Stern Radio Show," while still powerful, has suffered some ratings defeats. In the media centers of Los Angeles and New York, the show dropped in the winter quarter Arbitron rankings, released Monday, finishing behind AM all-news stations in both cities. In L.A., the show trailed KNX-AM (1070), placing seventh overall among morning-drive shows.

● *The Howard Stern Radio Show" can be heard weekday mornings on KLSX-FM (97.1) live from 3 to 6 a.m. with a rebroadcast from 6 to 10 a.m.*

out later it was pure coincidence, and I believe that, based on how I've always been treated since. When I came in, we talked about my dad immediately and got it out of the way. Again he had nothing but kind words and even admitted to feeling bad about how he had treated him.

Becoming a regular on the Stern show was a surprise to me. Suddenly my peers were midgets, prostitutes, crackheads, and women that would participate in contests to win fake boobs. A married guy with kids and a receding hairline seemed a little out of place. Maybe it's that I don't cheat on my wife, I love my kids, and yet I have an incurable dark side that I'm not afraid to talk about, just like him.

The night before I make an appearance on the show I think about what I would be embarrassed to tell a good friend. From there I just tell the truth and let Howard do his magic with the interview. I've disclosed things that I never could have if I knew there was a chance my mother would be listening, which she was not. For that reason I am including the most lurid in this book lest she miss out.

I've gotten massages regularly for years because of a neck injury from high school that continually acts up. One morning my wife gave me a coupon we'd received in the mail for a new Thai massage parlor. It seemed legit so I thanked my wife and headed over.

Halfway through the massage, the front door burst open and two Santa Monica police officers came charging in. The tables were separated by curtains which the police immediately pulled back. Thai women began screaming and one ran out a side door into the alley. I can honestly say that up until that moment it had not even occurred to me that this place was a "jack shack." As it turns out, it was legitimate, but some of the workers were undocumented and that's what the crackdown was all about. But pulling my pants on while a police officer began asking me my name and where I lived felt like a scene out of a Jim Norton book. Only in the book, Jim would still be demanding that the masseuse give him a happy ending.

I quickly removed the coupon from my pants pocket, showing it to the police officer and explaining that my wife had sent me here. He seemed uninterested, given they were only here to check for illegal working papers (although he did have a smirk on his face at my pathetic explanation). As I walked back out onto Lincoln Boulevard, a crowd had formed around the two police cars whose lights were still flashing. They all looked at me and judged. Again I produced the coupon, yelling, "I have a coupon! My wife sent me!" I ducked into my car and drove home in shame.

The most revealing and scandalous story I ever revealed on Howard's show continues to be brought up on the air whenever he wants to bust my balls. When I got into college and was studying English and reading things by guys like Whitman, Thoreau, and then later Allen Ginsberg, there was a lot of romanticizing of homosexuality. I grew up listening to Mick Jagger and other rock stars rumored to have experimented with it as well. I can't remember ever having gay feelings toward another man, but intellectually it still remained something I hadn't really explored.

Sophomore year of college, I was (barely) walking home from the bars at about four in the morning. At the time, I was living near Fenway Park. Like every major city in the world, Boston had a small wooded area that was reserved for anonymous gay sex. In this case, it was called the Fenway. I headed in.

Tired of wondering, I decided to try an experiment to see what happened. As I crossed the perimeter of this magical fairyland, I was filled with fright, curiosity, and slight nausea from drinking for the past eleven hours. Within thirty seconds a man popped out from behind a tree like a magical gay elf. He stood there with his hands on his hips, looking at me as if to say, "Tada! Here I am." This was it. Not knowing the social graces of wooded areas late at night, I stared and let him take the lead as he unzipped his fly and held out his penis. But not just his penis—he also thought it important to release his balls. I stood there for I-don't-know-how-long while staring at this horrible-looking thing.

All I knew was that it was facing the wrong direction, it looked ridiculous, and I had absolutely no attraction to it. So now I knew I was not gay—but I was also still in the woods in the middle of the night with a strange man standing in front of me with his penis out. I got scared and did the only thing I really knew how to do: pushed him as hard as I could. He tripped and fell over backward, rolled over onto his feet, and darted back into the mysterious darkness. I stumbled out of the woods and walked home, confident in my heterosexuality, but still a little confused about life in general. I've kept journals my whole life, and that night the entry in the black-marble-covered Mead notebook said simply: "What happened tonight didn't happen. I will never do that again." Oh, the shame . . .

Though that incident had happened many years earlier, I had never shared it with anyone except my wife, and that was only weeks before sharing it live on the air. It was incredibly freeing to let go of something that ultimately meant nothing, but that I had kept secret for so long.

Becoming a part of the Stern world requires a delicate balance between respecting your family and delivering good radio. Often one side loses. Recently, Erin has been putting the brakes on some of the things I say on the air. Like Kevin Meaney telling me when I first started that I should work clean, this felt wrong to me. She is right though, and this is part of my choice to both do what I love for a living, but remain committed to my family. My two kids are getting older and their friends' parents listen to the

2008 Porn Awards cohosts Tera Patrick and Greg Fitzsimmons. I am on the left (of her two tits).

things I say on *Stern* and other shows. That being said, Erin respects what I do and trusts that I will use my best judgment, no matter how bad it happens to be.

In 2008 I stood onstage before seven thousand porn stars and their fans as I hosted *The 25th Annual AVN Porn Awards* on Showtime. An hour later, I was in a suite at the top of a Vegas hotel washing down 10 milligrams of Vicodin with a nonalcoholic beer. Three feet away, my beautiful wife says good night to our five- and eight-year-old kids on the phone. She sounds a little on edge; it's the first time she's not been there to put them to bed. Also, there is a rumor that some of the porn stars are about to have an orgy.

A chubby man with illogically high self-esteem approaches us. I turn to Erin and say something that no man's wife should ever have to hear: "Honey, you know Ron Jeremy." Sadly, she does.

Rather than two realities crashing into each other, for me this all

Porn royalty Ron Jeremy holds court.

I remember a photo of my dad hosting the 1971 Miss New Jersey Shore Pageant; not exactly the Porn Awards. I think the fireman on the left won.

somehow folds into one. If this sounds like a contradiction, this was in fact the next logical step in a career loosely based on my father's, but updated to the twenty-first century.

My wife was by my side throughout the porn awards; not because she didn't trust me, but because she actually enjoys spending time with me. Las Vegas was a clash of cultures that particular weekend because the Consumer Electronics Convention is held at the same time as the Porn Convention. I've never seen so many women that every guy wants to fuck and so many guys that nobody wants to fuck. That's the beauty of porn: there's something for everyone.

I was, surprisingly, not very turned on by the whole thing. I was seeing the business side and it made it all seem kind of cold. Besides, my taste in porn has calmed down a lot since I was young. As a twenty-year-old, I resented any dialogue or attempt at a story whatsoever. I just wanted the sex.

Now that I'm forty-four, I kind of want the story. Who are these two? How did they meet? Are they in love? Will the Japanese girl's parents approve of these three giant black guys? I ended up hosting the show twice and then Erin and I decided that it might be best to move on. Mostly Erin on that particular decision.

On the not-so-sleazy side of things, I had received a letter from Boston University. My gut reaction was "Shit! I'm in trouble again!" I have performed every year since I graduated at an alumnus comedy show for the graduating students and their families. I helped create the event the year after graduation and look forward to going back each time to attack the school administration and explain to the parents what their kids have really been doing for the past four years. Some families bring their teenage children, and on this night, many of them pick up new vocabulary. Was I finally being punished for this? *Au contraire . . .*

I was being given the Distinguished Alumni Award. I was the youngest alumnus ever to receive it. I mailed the letter to my mom and drove her up to Boston for the ceremony.

At the awards dinner, I did twenty minutes on what a tool the school president John Silber was. I then admitted that I hadn't even applied to the school. The faculty cheered.

Afterward, my mom told me that my dad would have been proud. She told me the story of my father hosting a charity event for All Hallows High School. This was the Catholic high school he attended, and he started the night by asking for a show of hands by anyone who'd had the shit kicked out of them by Brother Ryan. Most of the hands went up as Brother Ryan, now an old man, shrank from the laughter.

I know that was a sweet moment for my Dad. I'm learning as I get older that you don't always have to take revenge; sometimes, if you wait long enough, life will do it for you. Detective Reggiano, the ferocious juvenile detective in Tarrytown, got a delicious dose of this himself. As it turned out, he had allegedly come home drunk one night and fell asleep next to his wife. She allegedly took this as an opportunity to superglue his penis to his leg, paying particular attention to lay a drop on the tip to seal the thing shut. I couldn't have asked for a sweeter punch line. Fighting back had

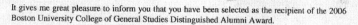

Boston University

College of General Studies
871 Commonwealth Avenue
Boston, Massachusetts 02215

March 24, 2006

Mr. Gregory Fitzsimmons
2009 Oakwood Avenue
Venice, CA 90291-3810

Dear Mr. Fitzsimmons:

It gives me great pleasure to inform you that you have been selected as the recipient of the 2006 Boston University College of General Studies Distinguished Alumni Award.

The Distinguished Alumni Award, given annually, is the most prestigious recognition conferred by CGS Alumni Association and has been presented to fewer than thirty CGS alumni. The selection committee consisted of your fellow alumni in the College of General Studies Alumni Association with recommendations by Dean Linda Wells. Your outstanding service to your profession, community, and alma mater set you high above the rest of the nominees this year.

The awards will be presented on Friday evening, May 12, 2006, during Reunion and Commencement Weekend at a reception and dinner attended by alumni, students, faculty, and family members. Under the bylaws of the CGS Alumni Association, recipients must be present at the ceremony to accept their awards. In addition, we invite you to attend BU Night at the Pops on Saturday, May 13, although I understand you will be hosting your annual Comedy Night for Boston University alumni and their families.

I sincerely hope you will honor us by accepting this award. If you accept this award, you will be the youngest GGS alumni award recipient in the College's history. If you have any questions, please contact Kirsten Lundeen, CGS Development and Alumni Officer, at 617/353-2891.

On behalf of more than 20,000 College of General Studies alumni, I congratulate you on this outstanding honor and look forward to seeing you in a few months.

Sincerely,

Daniel Bernstein

Daniel Bernstein, CGS '88/COM '90
President, CGS Alumni Association

cc: Dean Linda Wells

always been so automatic, I was starting to understand that it was often just sabotage.

I remembered a story from one of my religious education classes about Jacob fleeing his homeland in fear of his father and older brother after screwing them over. Years later when Jacob built up the courage to return home, he dreamt he was battling an angel who he was only able to defeat once he stopped fighting him. He realized that the angel was himself, and that he'd been fighting him his whole life instead of accepting that he needn't (did I seriously just use the word *needn't*? I'm a douche).

There is no simple happy ending to this story. I continue to work on my anger and issues with authority. Sometimes I regress. This book is an attempt to understand this cycle so I can stop it before it spreads to my own children. After all, I'm in charge of them. But how do you teach a child what you never really learned yourself? I like to think that I have painstakingly balanced the responsibilities of being a great dad and faithful husband with the ridiculous immaturity that my career as a professional buffoon requires.

There are moments that make me think I might be stretching this premise a little too thin. Without a castrating wife in my life to rein things in, I am left to make moral decisions in somewhat of a vacuum. Interviewing the very talented Jimmy Kimmel on my radio show one night, I asked, "What does a guy like me need to do to become a guy like you?" He said, "Don't host things like the Porn Awards."

I think he was considering the damage to my reputation, but turning the gig down would have also saved me a lot of unnecessary drama. Sitting in the front row directly in front of me, wearing dark sunglasses and a leather jacket, was rock star Dave Navarro from Jane's Addiction and the Red Hot Chili Peppers. His head was turned slightly away from me. The fact that I was destroying 99 percent of the room started to mean very little because there was one person in my eye line who was giving me no respect. I said nothing onstage, but a couple of weeks later during an appearance on *The Howard Stern Show,* I started to lay into the man I began calling "Mexican Prince." I talked about how he represented everything I hated about men in Los Angeles: eyeliner, hair products, and a cooler-than-thou attitude that comes off as very douchey.

I felt justified in attacking Navarro for breaking what I felt was a performers' code to respect one another onstage. Coincidentally, Dave Navarro
made an appearance on Howard's show about a month later. Howard took
the liberty of playing him a tape of my comments. He responded by calling
me a cunt and saying that he was just trying to enjoy the show and doesn't
remember having insulted me. I then went on my radio show and on *The
Adam Carolla Radio Show* and challenged Navarro to a fight: boxing, mixed
martial arts. I was giving Dave Navarro the choice. Looking back on this
now, I'm fairly sure that this marked the beginning of my midlife crisis.
Navarro blogged about me, and I continued challenging him, until, as fate
would have it, we crossed paths again on the set of a television show.

Comedian Dave Attell asked me to be the head writer on his version of
The Gong Show for Comedy Central. One of my jobs on tape day was to go
through the list of performers with the celebrity judges, one of whom was
Dave Navarro. I sent an olive branch back to his dressing room in the form
of a very hot prize girl who, as luck would have it, had already had sex with
Dave Navarro. What are the odds? The olive branch was slapped to the
ground. *Fine,* I thought, *let him think of jokes about a man who plays the trumpet
with his asshole all by himself.*

During a commercial break I was chatting with Navarro's fellow judges
Andy Dick and Triumph the Insult Comic Dog when we finally made eye
contact. After an awkward moment, Navarro looked at me and said, "So,
you still want to fight me?" We both started laughing and explained to
Triumph what had happened. Triumph brokered peace merely by saying,
"Maybe you two should share a peace pipe. And by that I mean blow Andy
Dick." We hung out after the show, and, later on, I got a text from Dave saying how much he enjoyed meeting me and that he was glad we had put the
fight behind us. I invited him on my radio show, and we've stayed in touch
ever since.

Most of my recent bad judgments involve separating my home life from
the insane things that happen in the Stern world. I recently had porn star
Belladonna in the radio studio behind my house doing a live broadcast of
my show on Howard Stern's Sirius channel. This is not an issue with my
wife, who trusts that I can make mature decisions. As Belladonna sat naked

in a hot tub about eight feet from where my wife and kids were sleeping, I began to not trust my wife's judgment (of me).

The Dave Navarro incident was not the only time I had used *The Howard Stern Show* when I had an ax to grind. It felt natural; using humor has always been an equalizer when I feel threatened or intimidated. The *Stern* show is a natural place to do this because it is good for the show, and it gets results.

In 2008 Artie Lange and I were booked to perform at a place called the West Palm Beach Cultural Center. We arrived the night of the show to find that the cultural center was actually a large circus tent pitched in what was now a muddy field, since the rain had not let up for three days. A second show had been billed and tickets had been sold, not taking into account the

Belladonna on *The Greg Fitzsimmons Show*. (Bra is always optional.)

fact that the promoter had not asked the acts if they wanted to do a second show. Artie did not. So now we had angry people lined up in the rain because they'd combined both shows into one.

I chronicled the entire experience on a broadcast of my own show on Howard's channel called *The Greg Fitzsimmons Show.* (I thought of that myself.) The Howard 100 news team picked up on the story and dug deep. Pressure was put on the West Palm Beach Cultural Center to pay up the money it had stiffed us that night. The Florida newspapers were soon running the story, and within two weeks, the promoter was being investigated by the Florida State Attorney General's office. A week after that, the West Palm Beach Cultural Center was put out of business. It turns out that it had been stiffing other people, but because of *The Howard Stern Show,* the comedians ended up receiving full payment—and we all got a great show from the experience.

When it comes to my mental health and emotional stability, there are very few people in the Greater Los Angeles area who have not been paid by me or my insurance company over the last ten years. My doctor recently suggested that part of my problem could be a sleep disorder and referred me to a clinic at Santa Monica Hospital. I arrived late for my ten o'clock check-in only to find out that I'd parked my car in the wrong garage and needed to go move it. I went around the corner in my pajamas, drove my car up to the cashier booth, and realized that I had left my ticket back at the sleep study center. I pleaded my case, but the attendant showed me zero understanding. He told me that without the ticket, I would need to pay him $60 cash.

I explained to him that I would not be paying him $60 cash, and he told me that I would. I asked to speak to his supervisor, at which point the attendant ceased to have the ability to speak English. I asked him to check the security camera at the gate where I'd come in and he would see that I had just showed up ten minutes earlier. When he told me there was no security camera at the gate where I pulled in, I bid him a fine evening and put my car in reverse, winding backward the wrong way toward the gate I'd entered.

I pulled up short of the wooden barrier and put the car in park. A couple of nurses heading home stopped and looked on in stunned silence as a man in pajamas began tugging at a ten-foot wooden barrier. After about a minute, my effort paid off with a loud crack. I placed the barrier down gently on the side of the ramp and drove my car to the correct parking garage. Thirty minutes later, I was hooked up to a brain monitor and drifting into a beautiful sleep. I really hope the security guard at that parking garage in Santa Monica does not read this book. If he does, it will prove that he speaks perfectly good English.

People who know me today are often surprised when they witness first-hand the anger that lies mostly dormant in me at this point in my life. My friend Will Hayes, who's an alcoholic, was in the passenger seat of my car one day as we drove down my street in Venice. Up ahead we could see a car coming toward us that seemed to swerve into the cars ahead to intimidate them and get more lane space. When he did it to me, I handed Will my coffee and calmly said, "Would you mind holding this for a moment?" Throwing the car in reverse, I floored it and politely but firmly drove the gentleman to the side of the road. I stepped out of the car and approached him (still very calmly) before beginning to punch him in the face. The driver backed out and took off, at which point I got back in my car, asked Will for my coffee, and continued on to the hardware store.

I soon started seeing a therapist about road rage following several more incidents. While driving my son, Owen, to school when he was five, I had to swerve to the side of the road because of a car taking a turn too wide and encroaching into my lane. As I slammed on the brakes, I hit the horn, and the driver gave me the finger. I jumped out of my car and punched his window, but he continued on down Palm Avenue as I stood in the middle of the street waving for him to come back. Owen sat in the backseat looking out the window, observing another great Fitzsimmons tradition.

Two weeks later, while I was drinking a juice box and watching children bounce on an inflatable SpongeBob SquarePants float, a friend from the neighborhood came over and said hello. He was one of the creators of the TV show *Lost*. After some small talk, he hesitantly told me that *he* was the driver who had cut me off and driven away. We laughed, but it was awkward and weird.

There are times when I wish I could have stayed in a job longer, stayed in school longer, stayed in a bar longer. There is a reason why I make my living alone, following only the guidelines that I stay up onstage for an hour and that I make people laugh. There is no dress code, morality code, or language restriction. It's actually a sign of success if a few customers each weekend ask for their money back because they're offended. There is a reason why I make my living in my garage studio, holding a microphone and talking to whomever I invite to sit down with me that week—or all by myself. Along the way I've learned to actually hold down writing jobs and really enjoy them. But professionally, there is no contest; stand-up is the girl that brought me to the dance, and it is the one I will go home with at the end of the night.

I never got into stand-up to help people or make them feel good; it's always selfishly been about me. The exception is when I get the chance to do comedy benefits. Ten years ago, after losing a dear friend to Spinal Meningitis, I helped start a foundation to raise money through benefit shows. Gerry "Red" Wilson was truly an everyman, having grown up in Queens where he taught school when he began doing stand-up. Before dying, Gerry saw great success with several big television deals and an unforgettable moment on *The Tonight Show* where he proposed to his girlfriend Kathleen. She and Gerry's cousins work with me to keep his spirit alive with a show that makes the area around Town Hall each year look like a miniature St. Patrick's Day Parade as it spills over with his friends, family, and former students. As a matter of fact, Gerry's uncle Denis recently served as Grand Marshal of the New York St. Patrick's Day Parade. That's the honorary equivalent of an Italian guy being cast on "Jersey Shore."

Through this night I am brought back to what is great about the Irish; the loyalty, the laughter, and the desire to help others. My relatives sing Irish songs without any hint of irony and continue reciting the limericks my grandfather taught them many years before. As far back as I can remember, my family would stand on the side of Fifth Avenue and watch Florence march proudly with the Ancient Order of Hibernians.

But I became embarrassed later in life by the Irish stereotypes associated with drinking. This was of course after spending most of my life reinforcing it. Throw in a few bad priests, and I found myself turning my back on my

Irish identity. I was now taking it back. There was no better way to celebrate than getting my ass back to the parade!

My longtime friend Mike Gibbons's father, who knew my father from playing pickup basketball games when they were teenagers, was to be this year's Grand Marshal. I was invited to join him at the front of the line holding a banner that said "Friends and Family of the Grand Marshal." I found out later he couldn't get anyone from his own lazy family to hold it, but nonetheless I felt proud of Mr. Gibbons and proud of my people.

I've gone back many times to reclaim things from my past that I had rejected too easily. Raising children requires that you go back not only to see what was wrong with your own childhood, but to draw from the things that shaped your character in the first place. In my life it has often been very difficult to differentiate one from the other. I only hope that my own children will look back and have good, wholesome memories from childhood to offset the absolute trauma that will result from their reading of this book.

My Loin Fruit

"I'm serious! Knock it off and go to bed! Now!"

—Me (last night)

When I tell people I am writing this book they invariably ask me the same question: "Why would your mother save all of these letters?" I do have a few theories:

1. She likes to laugh at how stupid I am.
2. She sees the letters as pins she can use to let the air out of my big ego whenever she sees fit.
3. Knowing how hard it is to raise insane kids, she believed I might one day find patterns in the letters that would help me in raising my own children. (She realized the high genetic probability of my children becoming assholes.)

Her prediction has come true as I am now saddled with two kids who mock everything I thought I'd figured out about myself. I am now confronted with the same challenge my parents once faced: How do you teach your kids to maintain a healthy, defiant attitude without bringing needless drama into their lives (and the lives of their parents)? How do I convince them to respect people in charge when they know I've made my living doing the opposite of that?

When I told my mom I was writing this book, she showed me many documents that I didn't even know existed. The one that stands out in my mind the most was not about my life, it was about hers. It illuminated so much about what she had experienced in her family and, over time, what had allowed her to forgive and let go. After the death of her father, Florence, she and her siblings were sorting through sixty years of stored documents in the attic. (Yes, we have come full circle. Thank you, Boston University English degree!) Her sister discovered a yellowed, very official-looking certificate that turned out to be their parents' marriage license.

Florence McCarthy and Margaret Harrington were married just five months prior to the birth of their oldest child. My mind flashed back to my mom's description of being attacked by her own mother in the maternity ward for the exact same transgression. By saving these documents, my family allows each generation to glimpse not only what came before, but what will likely come after.

I provided mom with a magnificent thank-you gift when she was visiting us last Thanksgiving. While throwing around a football with Owen, I dropped a perfectly thrown spiral and the prick laughed at me. He taunted me by saying, "Hey, Dad, you suck!" again and again; and a swell of validation came over my mom's face. Watching the football roll away from me amid the laughter of two superior generations of Fitzsimmonses, it dawned on me that a "revolution" refers not only to insurrection but also to the movement of things in a circle. Like a child running away and later wanting to come home. Or a football that should have been caught.

"Oh. I suck? Well, it's nice to see that I'm raising my father."

I started to wonder how long it would be before Owen started drinking and beating me.

Owen is big, strong, bright, and not intimidated in the least by his own dad. It truly is every father's deep seeded fear that (like Oedipus) your son will grow past you. Let's not dwell on that mother part . . . As I support and challenge him to be the best person he can be, I also fear him and mourn, in advance, the pain I know awaits him when he has rendered me obsolete. It is for this reason that I have made considerable effort to slow him down. Let's take a look back.

Over the last three generations, my family has ascended from peasants in famine-ravaged Ireland at the end of the last century to members of America's educated upper-middle class at the beginning of this one. There is little I can do in my lifetime to advance the family's lot, short of becoming president or having a scotch named after me.

Eleven years ago, this reality haunted me each night as I contemplated having gotten Erin pregnant. Had I earned the right to bring a new generation into this world? Do I have the resources to improve upon what has come before me? Or will I be responsible for the Fitzsimmons family socially and financially flatlining? Erin could tell I wasn't ready because I was still using condoms.

I'd heard about the new options available to couples wishing to have not only healthy babies but really fucking great ones. It is now possible to purchase a model's egg online. Having spent the early part of my life trying to get access to supermodel vagina, I can now have a piece of it shipped right to my house! Also available online (and I am not making this up): sperm from an Ivy League student. (Granted, the better students are likely *not* whacking off for cash, but the donors still got in. If they had paid me for beating off in college, I could have retired after senior year. Comfortably. One night, my roommate Brad offered me $25 to *not* jerk off. I told him to keep his filthy money. You can't put a price on joy.)

No longer limited to Darwin's shallow gene pool, I could upgrade my clan's pale, skinny, freckled DNA. Alcoholism is passed on like a recipe for emotional failure. By age twenty-five, our hairlines sprint for the back of our heads, followed by lesions on any strip of skin in contact with the sun. It suddenly seemed a disservice to just bust a nut the old-fashioned way. Someday, when he can't make the football team or pass ninth grade, he's going to resent me. "Thanks. It's been great watching the twenty-first century pass me by because you couldn't cough up five hundred dollars."

Pondering this opportunity, though, I knew that I would only be accelerating the inevitable challenge to my manhood. So I did it the same way my forefathers did: in a quiet shame-based missionary position with minimal eye contact. Why did I not do everything in my power to give my babies the best possible odds for success? Because if there's one thing my father taught me—and I'm sure his father taught him—keep your family in line.

I could afford to send my kids to a great private school here in Los Angeles. Or I could put money aside for my retirement (which by Hollywood standards should be kicking in within the next eighteen months). Look, public school wasn't good enough for me, and it will come up short for them, too. They are actually in an amazing public school that has a Spanish-language immersion program. Most of the students come from Spanish-speaking homes and are harder working, better behaved, and shorter than kids in private school. This not only exposes my children to a diverse and productive classroom environment, it almost guarantees them a spot on every athletic team.

It is important to me that my son is not a pussy. I get how my father felt about raising a son who is tough enough for this world. While fathers should not encourage their boys to be violent, there is a very deep satisfaction that comes from knowing that your son is capable of kicking someone's ass, should it be necessary. When Owen was about two years old, we went to Sea World in San Diego with comedian Jim Breuer and his family. It was a scorcher, and, having already taken in the performance of Shamu the killer whale and the female trainer who might or might not someday become his lunch, we were kicking back in the children's playground while the kids burned off their sugar high. A bigger boy, probably three and a half, decided that my son was done sitting on the rubber mushroom and shoved him off.

I took a breath, not wanting to rush to Owen's side, thereby bringing out tears that might otherwise have stayed in his eyeballs. What I saw next inspired me. Owen began a slow motion run after the three-and-a-half-year-old, now on to another playground activity. This was an insult not only to Owen, but also to the now empty rubber mushroom. Owen caught up to the boy, pulled him to the ground, and sat on his chest. It was like watching midget wrestling with the added fun of knowing that the midget is your own son.

I've never been a huge sports fan, but I get excited about the two teams my dad and I followed when I was young: the Mets and the Giants. Two years ago I sat down with Owen to watch the Giants play in Super Bowl

XLII. With a minute left and down by four points to the heavily favored New England Patriots, things looked doubtful for Big Blue. What happened next is considered by many to be the greatest Super Bowl reception of all time. Wide receiver David Tyree miraculously pinned a high pass against his helmet with one hand for a reception that kept the Giants drive alive. They went on to win, but at the moment Tyree held on to that ball while getting hammered by a defender, I jumped up so high that my head smashed against the light fixture in the ceiling. The next day I tried to replicate that height and fell short by about four inches. Owen joined me in screaming and yelling and we talked about the game nonstop for about a week. It was the 1986 World Series all over again.

Another recent experience connects the generations even more. Owen and I sometimes play backgammon and listen to the Mel Brooks and Carl Reiner album the *2,000 Year Old Man*. I had listened to the same album with my Dad when I was about Owen's age. Owen can recite most of the routines. While trick-or-treating last year I tapped Owen (sorry, Han Solo) on the shoulder and said, "Look, it's Mel Brooks!" He said, "Someone dressed as Mel Brooks?" I said, "No, it's *Mel Brooks!*" He spun around and there he was. Turns out his grandkid lives in the neighborhood and he was taking

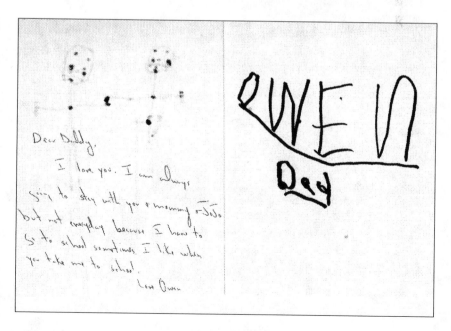

I like to play Trouble with you. I love you. You are special because you give me mints after cereal or candy.
Owen

I love you, daddy. I like when we go to places together. I like when you take care of me when mommy is not here. You are special because you are nice. Daddy, you give me the best fruit like melons and cantaloupe. Sometimes we are at restaurants you order for me. Happy Father's Day.

Love,
Owen

Happy father's day. Mom! Oh, I mean Dad. I hope you like the present I got you. I call it Pinky Monkey. Today is the last day of sncool. (I don't know the date.) I ♥ U The end... or not. To be contine blah blah blah...

him trick-or-treating. He cracked up when we told him Owen was a fan of his at nine years old.

(Note to my kids: I am publishing your notes to me not to embarrass you, but because they mean a lot to me and I want you to know that. They mark a time in your lives when you have nothing but love for me and express it often. Life can be strange and you may forget sometimes what family means, but now, at this moment, here is a snapshot of a time that I consider perfect.)

Let's move on to Josephine. Some people believe that children are like clay, and the parent molds the clay into the character of the person the child will become. While this might be partly true, it does not apply to redheads. Redheaded children are deranged. I know this because I have one named Josephine. As a matter of fact, I was one. I spent the first seven years of my life with deep orange hair. I still have this clown color in my pubes as a painful reminder of this nightmarish fact. Maybe we are treated differently and start to internalize a loneliness and sense of anger, or maybe it's just a warning for people to stay the fuck away from us.

This following story best sums up Josephine's personality. My family belongs to a country club in Marina del Rey. Let me rephrase that: my family has a key card to the pool of a nice corporate apartment in Marina del Rey. We stayed there during a renovation and continue to visit the pool on a regular basis. The tentative nature of this arrangement requires a certain level of restraint and respectability on the part of my family. I patiently teach them this behavior as we crash the establishment, because, after all, how else are they going to learn class?

Late one afternoon, I began the countdown to exiting the pool. JoJo was given a five-minute warning, a two-minute warning, and then asked to get out of the pool so we could head home. She seemed to have water in her ears because there was no acknowledgment that she had heard anything that I had said. My goal was very clear: having strategically flipped over in the sun for the past thirty minutes, my bathing suit was dry, and I wished to extricate my child from the pool without having to jump back in. This clearly was not going to happen. Switching tactics from the promise of treats to veiled threats, I was getting no response.

There are few things in life more humiliating than being observed by other adults as an incompetent parent. Parents enjoy the failure of other parents, because in that moment they feel like they are doing a better job than at least *one* moron. On this day, I was that moron. I finally jumped in the pool and removed JoJo firmly but within the boundaries of what would not be considered domestic violence. The sun had gone down, and it was chilly, but when JoJo asked for a dry towel, I refused to give it to her, instead telling her to put on her flip-flops and start walking to the car. I would never hit my kids, but the idea of inflicting other kinds of pain on them is fine with me. The car was parked one floor below and across a long underground parking garage. It was very cold, and JoJo's skin turned into a sea of pink goose bumps. Her lips were blue, and her teeth were chattering. If I were a better man I would tell you that I did not enjoy it. But I enjoyed it a great deal because I was winning. It felt unfair since I was a grown man, but this is how children learn. As we got to the car, I opened the door for JoJo and held out a dry, warm, pink towel. It had Dora the Explorer on it, her favorite. She pushed the towel back toward me and climbed into the car cold, wet, and shaking. I drove home glancing in the rearview mirror as she stared straight ahead, neither crying nor drying herself in any way. It was at that moment that I realized that if Owen didn't get me first, this little girl was going to destroy me.

Ironically, my biggest comfort is that JoJo is drawn to the Lord Jesus Christ. This is odd because we never go to church. I suspect she is already aware that she will need big help down the road, so she is going right to the top early on. Owen, on the other hand, is not a fan. My mother made the mistake of bringing him to church when he was only four. He found the place entertaining, as the choir sang in front of the stained-glass windows. Then his eyes came across the crucifix, in this case a particularly gory depiction of Jesus's corpse dripping blood from the head, wrists, and feet. My mother had to carry him crying from the church as he demanded, "Why does Cheese-its have 'ow-ies' on his hands and feet?"

I myself have issues, and since high school have put a lot of distance between me and religion. Walking into a church, though, still conjures a deep sense of awe and belonging. Triple that feeling and then double it again and you've got Sister Josephine, trembling before the altar. This past summer we visited the Cathedral of St. John the Divine in New York City. It is one of the largest and most inspired cathedrals in the world, and my wife happened to go to elementary school there (with fellow half-Jew Ben Stiller, so the admission standards were pretty lax).

Upon entering the cathedral, JoJo went to the prayer candles and lit one. I asked her who she was praying for. She said, "Your father. I wish I could have met him." She knelt beside the prayer candles with her hands in prayer position and her head down. As we sat down closer to the altar, she asked me about the Transfiguration of Jesus's body and blood and why people eat it. Owen went pale and stepped outside for a little air.

She continued, asking about Jesus's Ascension and the relationship of the Holy Trinity. "What's purgatory and is it different from Heaven and Hell?" When I got home I called my godmother, Ann Ward, for advice on this spiritual conflict before me. Knowing about my falling out with the Church, Ann was overjoyed to learn that my daughter was now a true believer. I asked Ann how she had maintained a relationship with an institution that was so rigid and judgmental. She told me that the Church is what she grew up with, and the sacraments mean something to her.

She shared with me the story of her mother's funeral. Many of her friends were Jewish, Muslim, or none of the above. She was concerned they would not be allowed to receive Communion. The priest had known Ann for years, and was involved with a lot of the work she'd done in the community. That day, Communion was opened up to all who wanted to share in it. Though moved by this lesson on passing through life not fighting what you could easily just exist beside, I continue choosing to engage all conflict wherever it may present itself. It's been working for me so far . . .

One afternoon I was given a note at school after my little angel had climbed on the roof during lunch. After being told repeatedly by a woman to come down, she refused, saying, "You're not even my teacher."

After delivering a pointless and ignored lecture about needing to respect adults, I asked her, "Why do you think you get into trouble so often?" Without even hesitating, she made a face and said, "Because of *the rules.*"

Before sending her to her room as punishment, I tried to reach out and reassure her that she is not a bad person.

"You may get in trouble sometimes, but you know that I'll always love you. There's nothing you can do that would make me not still love you."

"What if I killed your mother?"

(Pause.)

"How would you kill my mother?"

"Riley's dad has a sword above his fireplace."

"You would never kill Grandma."

"No." JoJo thinks for a moment. "Not unless she makes me really angry."

I send her to her room so that I can call a priest, warn my mother, and try to line up road work for the next decade or so. Twenty minutes later, confounded by what is going through her mind, I sneak around the side of the house and look in her window. I need to know how she is affected by what has just happened. She's put a Polynesian CD into her boom box from a Hawaiian-themed party we'd had for her birthday. She's cross-legged on her bed wearing a lei—motionless, except for her eyes. They are a deep green, and the left one has a perfect rim of gold around the pupil. They dart in all directions as if neurons are exploding. She's processing the weaknesses

---

Edison Language Academy/ Academia de idiomas Edison
Discipline Form/ Forma disciplinaria

Name/ Nombre: Josephine Fitsimmons **Date/ Fecha:** 5/22/09 **Time/ Hora:** 12:10

Teacher/ Maestra/o: Rankin **Room/ Salón:** 27 **Grade/ Grado:** K

Referred by/ Persona refiriendo: Sergio Rodriguez

Reason/ Razón: (circle/ haga un círculo alrededor)

Repeated Teasing or Name Calling/ Burla continua   Bullying/ Intimidando   Stealing/ Robando   Other/ Otro _____

Boundary Rule/ Fuera del lugar autorizado   Physically hurting another student/ Lastimando a alguien físicamente

Destruction of Property/ Destrucción de propiedad   Refusing to follow directions/ Negarse a seguir las instrucciones

Explanation/ Explicación: Un-safe behavior. Doing gymnastics in the bathroom (flips)

Steps already taken/ Pasos tomados: (circle and date/ haga un círculo alrededor y escriba la fecha)

Discussion /Conversación   In class consequence/ Consecuencia en la clase   Sit and think/ Sentarse y pensar

Time in another classroom/ Tiempo en otro salón   Teacher mediation/ Mediación de la maestra/o

Call or conference with parents/ Llamar o tener conferencia con los padres

Cool Tools redirection/ Repaso de las Herramientas Chéveres   Other/ Otro _____

Action taken by the adult/ Acción que tomó el adulto Sent to the office for conference with the principal. Next time they'll lose recess.

Next steps/ Siguientes pasos Please reinforce w/ JoJo the basic safety rules @ school

Signature/ Firma _____ **date/ fecha** 5/22/09

Parent signature/ Firma de padres _____ **date/ fecha** _____

Unsafe behavior: gymnastics in the bathroom.

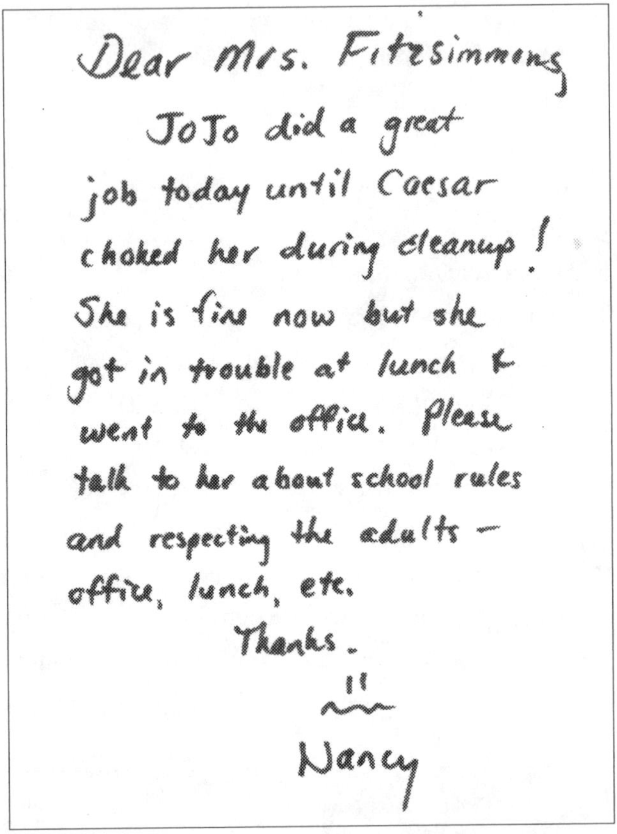

Dear Mrs. Fitesimmons

JoJo did a great job today until Caesar choked her during cleanup! She is fine now but she got in trouble at lunch & went to the office. Please talk to her about school rules and respecting the adults — office, lunch, etc.

Thanks.

Nancy

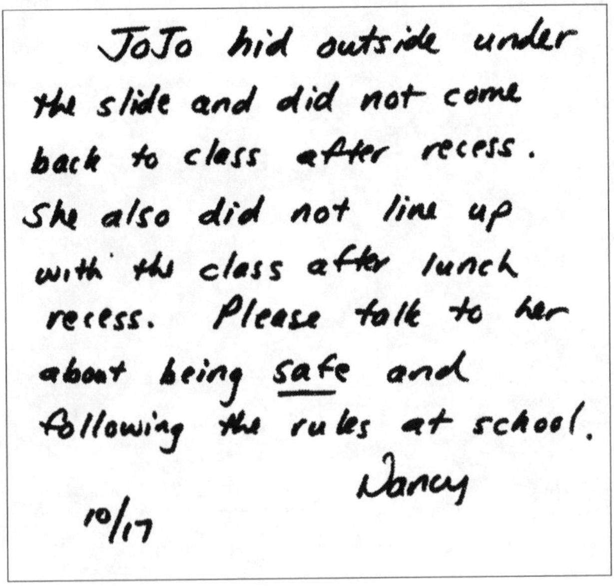

JoJo hid outside under the slide and did not come back to class after recess. She also did not line up with the class after lunch recess. Please talk to her about being <u>safe</u> and following the rules at school.

Nancy

10/17

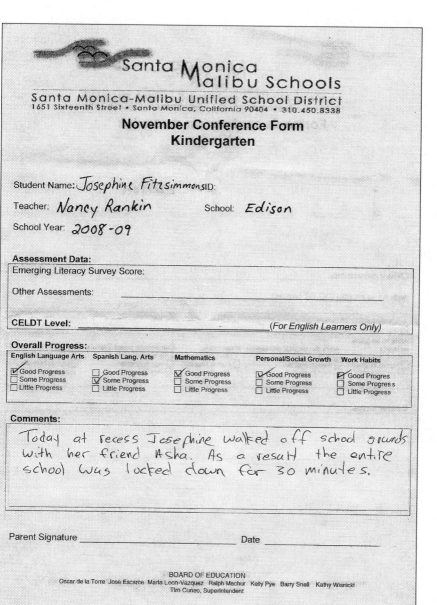

Santa **M**onica
Malibu Schools

Santa Monica-Malibu Unified School District
1651 Sixteenth Street • Santa Monica, California 90404 • 310.450.8338

November Conference Form
Kindergarten

Student Name: *Josephine Fitzsimmons* ID:

Teacher: *Nancy Rankin*   School: *Edison*

School Year: *2008-09*

Assessment Data:

Emerging Literacy Survey Score:

Other Assessments:

CELDT Level: _____ *(For English Learners Only)*

Overall Progress:

English Language Arts	Spanish Lang. Arts	Mathematics	Personal/Social Growth	Work Habits
☑ Good Progress	☐ Good Progress	☑ Good Progress	☑ Good Progress	☑ Good Progres
☐ Some Progress	☑ Some Progress	☐ Some Progress	☐ Some Progress	☐ Some Progres s
☐ Little Progress	☐ Little Progress	☐ Little Progress	☐ Little Progress	☐ Little Progress

Comments:

Today at recess Josephine walked off school grounds
with her friend Asha. As a result the entire
school was locked down for 30 minutes.

Parent Signature _____ Date _____

I've just betrayed to her in my hollow attempt at discipline. She is stronger now, and we both know that time is her only constraint. Eventually I will be forced to run away from my own home. The new data processed, her eyes show resolve and drift heavily to one corner of the room. Conversely, her limbs begin to move. She stands and begins—subtly, elegantly—to do a hula dance. I slip away on wobbly legs.

Later on, as Erin grips the rolled-up note like it is the baton in an eternal relay race of bad genetics, I give her a hug. "Congratulations. You're the new Mrs. Fitzsimmons!"

Acknowledgments

Howard Stern; Kerri Kolen, David Rosenthal, Kate Ankofski, Alexis Welby, Jonathan Karp, Aileen Boyle, Nina Pajak, Jackie Seow, Jonathan Evans, Ruth Lee-Mui; Rob Goodman; Peter Steinberg; Patricia Fitzsimmons, Bobby Fitzsimmons; Deirdre Gale; Michael O'Brien; Jim McLure; Frank Sebastiano; Chris Jennings; Gary Dell'Abate; Eddie Brill; the amazing teachers at Rye Country Day School; Boston University; Rich Super; Ann Ward; Jared Levine; Alex Kohner; BKMY Law; The Friars Club; Eleanor Seigler; Adam Carolla; Sarah Silverman; Will, Scott, Sal & Richard, Ronnie, Shuli, Ted, Brian, Jared; Zach Galifianakis; Tim Sabean; Steve Langford; Andy Richter; Alan Haldeman; Artie Lange; Brad Driver; Matt Rice; Jimmy Kimmel; Joe Rogan; Johnny Trouble & Mags; Louis C.K.; Morrow Jones; Robin Quivers; Alex Gardner; Dave Attell; Harvey Altman and Company; Dave Navarro; David Letterman; Fred Norris; Mike August; Mike Cioffi; Justin Edbrooke; John Hein; Kevin Meaney; Lee Kernis; Lisa G; Myspace Comedy; The Hoynes Family; Tom O'Neil; The Gale Family; Ruthanne Secunda; Sarah "Fearless" Feron; Scott & Mia Bass; "Sneaky" Pete Carrs; The Bob & Tom Show; the Gibbons family; Gibbs, Pete, Duds, Cocktail Man, Brix, Johnny, The Senator, Ted, Billy C, Rube, Sam & Tim, Mase, Jean & Paul; the

McCarthy family; the Mulligan family; the Kovel family; Danielle Stewart; Chris Schuler; Cindy Comito; iTunes; Bruce Hills; Bubba the Love Sponge; Chari Adrian; Charlene Barretto; Jonathon Davis; Jonny Weiss; Kathleen Lyons; Chelsea Handler; Chris & Tess Mcguire; the Conan O'Brien show; Dave Rath; Don Buchwald; Don Gavin; Donny Miraje; Eric Leiderman; Estee; Freddy Roman; Gail Gilchrist; Jason Burns; Jay & Tony; Jean-Pierre Trebot; Jenny Jedeiken; Jeff Wills; Jessica Mcmullen; Brett Shurman; Matt Malloy; Michael Caputo; Michael Ciarlente; Brian Meyer; Jill Leiderman; Mary Patterson Broome; Mike Dugan; Kevin Nealon; Kitt Boss; Kristin Newman; Len & Heather Cariou; Louis Faranda; Caroline Hirsch; Marc & Scott Krantz; Al Rosenberg; Alan Zweibel; Mary Fitzgerald; Cori Lahners; Tom Arnold; Tom & Roslyn Debow; Dana Gould; Mary Jo Buttafuco; Mike Mills; Mike Royce; Jill Schwartz; Jim Ackerman; Keith Robinson; Molly Shminke; Patrick Avedisian; Phil Mazo; Rolleen Heinman; Dave Becky; Ross Brockley; Steve Cohen; Zoe Friedman; Billy Burr; Wanda Sykes; Suzy Aarons; the McGovern family; the Reed family; the Kelleher family; the Stout family; Todd Yasui; Beth Osisek; Lisa Leingang; Tom Cotter; Aura Sotaj; Bart Coleman; Tracey Katsky; Vinny Brand; Upright Citizens Brigade; Vivian Sorenson; Mark Babbit; Adam & Rocky Dubin; Andy Dick; Rick Newman; Ann Maney; Tricia (Irish America); Lori Orum; Beena Kamlani

In Memory Of:

Bob Fitzsimmons; Frank McCarthy; Gerry Red Wilson; Tommy Bucci; Mr. John Meaney; Glenn Robertson; Kevin Knox; Veronica Manzella; Rich Jeni; Bill Hicks; George Carlin; Robert Schimmel; Greg Giraldo

Permissions and Illustration Credits

(Illustrations not listed are courtesy of Greg Fitzsimmons)

Barton Silverman/ *The New York Times*/ Redux: 90

Courtesy of Worldwide Pants: 156

The Hollywood Reporter article used with permission of e5 Global Media, LLC: 157 (top left)

The Journal News (Westchester): 157 (top right)

Courtesy of *Time Out New York*, March 6–13, 1997: 158

Copyright © 2001 Los Angeles Times, Paul Brownfield. Reprinted with Permission: 178

Ethan Miller / Getty Images Entertainment / Getty Images: 181

Printed in the United States
By Bookmasters